FAT-FREE DESSERTS

Quick-and-easy mouthwatering recipes

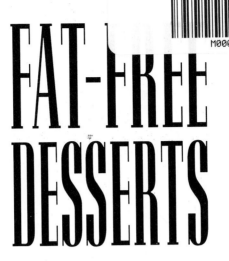

KAREN L. PELLEGRIN, PH.D.

CB
CONTEMPORARY BOOKS
A TRIBUNE NEW MEDIA COMPANY

Library of Congress Cataloging-in-Publication Data

Pellegrin, Karen L.
    Fat-free desserts : quick-and-easy, mouthwatering recipes /
Karen L. Pellegrin.
        p.   cm.
    Includes index.
    ISBN 0-8092-3444-0
    1. Low-fat diet—Recipes.   2. Desserts.   I. Title.
RM237.7.P45   1995
641.5′638—dc20   95-2785
                                                                    CIP

To Chris.

You are the icing on my cake.

Cover design by Ginny Pitre-Hay
Cover and page 87 photograph by Chris Cassidy
All other interior photos courtesy of the *Chicago Tribune*

Featured on the cover: Chocolate Fudge Layer Cake

Copyright © 1995 by Karen L. Pellegrin, Ph.D.
All rights reserved
Published by Contemporary Books, Inc.
Two Prudential Plaza, Chicago, Illinois 60601-6790
Manufactured in the United States of America
International Standard Book Number: 0-8092-3444-0
10   9   8   7   6   5   4

Contents

♠

Acknowledgments

♦

Special thanks to:

My honest and enthusiastic taste-testing panel, especially those at the Medical University of South Carolina Weight Management Center and the VA PTSD Clinical Team in Charleston, SC, who took the time to taste and critique my desserts. Your feedback made this a better cookbook.

My husband, Chris Frueh, who was there from the beginning of my search for fat-free desserts, for being patient and supportive and for enduring a chronically catastrophic kitchen and nine weeks of chocolate cheesecake during the completion of this cookbook.

My parents, Judy and Gene Pellegrin, who have always believed in me, for keeping the house stocked with love and sweets.

My sisters, Becky Padavan and Lauren Wetter, for being dear friends.

My agent, Alice Martell, for your hard work, enthusiasm, and support and for making this cookbook a piece of cake.

Gene Brissie, Linda Gray, and Contemporary Books for putting it all together.

1

Introduction

♠

Why This Cookbook Is Unique

What do my recipes for Double Chocolate Brownies, Cherry-Vanilla Cream Pie, and Coconut-Fudge Swirl Cheesecake have in common? Besides tasting rich, moist, and decadent, these and all of the recipes in this cookbook contain less than one-half gram of fat per generous serving.

How do my dessert recipes differ from others that are low-fat or fat-free? Until now, such recipes have fallen into one of two categories:

Tasty-but-not-too-healthy: Some cookbooks feature recipes that are only moderately low in fat and contain ingredients such as egg yolks, butter, cream cheese, and oils. If you eat desserts regularly and are concerned about your health, such recipes are only a small improvement over the higher-fat versions.

Healthy-but-not-too-tasty: Other recipes succeed in being heart-healthy and fat-free, they just aren't decadent. The basic problem with healthy-but-not-too-tasty recipes is that their creators fell prey to the pervasive "sugar myths." Despite a wealth of research that disputes the sugar myths, most people still believe that sugar is bad for them; that honey, fructose, and other such sweeteners are significantly better for them than refined sugar; or both.

The purpose of this cookbook is to introduce a new category of desserts:

Great-tasting, fat-free desserts: The recipes in *Fat-Free Desserts* are fat-free *and* delicious because they contain virtually no high-fat ingredients, yet they don't sacrifice the flavor that sugar provides. Almost all of these recipes call for white, brown, or powdered sugars, which are no more *or less* nutritious than the so-called natural sugars such as honey and concentrated fruit that other low-fat cookbooks tend to prescribe.

Although sugar has little significant nutritional value, current research indicates that eating sugar is not harmful to your health. Most desserts are unhealthy because of their high *fat* content. A high-fat diet has been associated with serious, life-threatening conditions such as heart disease and several forms of cancer. Because of this, health experts recommend that we significantly reduce our fat intake—particularly our saturated fat intake—and consume no more than 30 percent of our daily calories in the form of fat. Many experts recommend a diet of only 20 percent of calories from fat.

While most people in this country are more likely to eat too much fat, it is possible to eat too little fat. Because our bodies cannot produce the essential fatty acids we need to live, we must consume them to stay healthy. Therefore, although there are no generally accepted recommendations regarding minimum fat intake, it is *not* healthy to strive for a completely fat-free diet.

A healthy diet is low in fat, high in fiber, and rich in fruits and vegetables. For more information on maintaining a healthy diet, consult a registered dietitian.

Facts About Weight Management

The recipes in this cookbook were not created to be low in calories; however, they are lower in calories than equivalent recipes made with fat, and some of them contain less than 200 calories per generous serving. Despite all the diet fads, myths, and "miracle cures" promoted, the process of gaining weight is fairly simple and predictable. If you eat fewer calories than your body burns in energy, you will lose weight. If you eat more calories than your body burns, you will gain weight. If you eat and burn the same number of calories, you will maintain your weight. It takes an excess or a deficit of 3,500 calories to gain or lose one pound.

Fat is an extremely dense source of calories. It has more than twice the calories per gram as either carbohydrates (including sugar) or protein (fat has 9 calories per gram; carbohydrates and protein have 4 calories per gram). Reducing your fat intake while maintaining a healthy intake of carbohydrates and protein is therefore a good way to reduce your daily caloric intake. Even on a very low-fat diet, however, it is still possible to eat more calories than your body burns in energy. That's why it's important to count calories, not just fat grams, when trying to lose weight.

Diet is only one side of the weight-management coin, of course. Exercise is the other, and perhaps more important, side. Several studies have found that exercise is the single most important behavior in the successful maintenance of weight loss. Exercise not only burns calories, it also preserves muscle tissue. This is important because muscle tissue burns a lot of calories even when you are not exercising; fat tissue does not. Regular exercise has also been found to reduce the risk for a myriad of diseases, improve mood, and reduce stress. In reality, regular exercise is the closest thing there is to a miracle cure for obesity!

If you need help managing your weight, consult a registered

dietitian, an exercise physiologist, or a psychologist who has expertise in this area. Always consult your physician before beginning an exercise program.

The Inspiration for This Cookbook

While all humans are born with a preference for sweet tastes, a characteristic that evolved most likely because it encouraged consumption of nutritious fruits, I seemed to develop a stronger sweet preference than most! My wonderful parents always had the kitchen stocked with a variety of sweet treats; Cap'n Crunch cereal, Hostess Ding Dongs, and ice cream were staples. I loved learning to bake with my mom, and I loved my Saturday sundae outings with my dad. I always felt sorry for kids whose parents placed restrictions on their intake of sweets.

In college, although we had no idea how to cook regular meals, my roommate and I were quite proud of our incredibly tasty but obscenely high-fat cookie creations. At the time, I didn't know much about the role of nutrition in health and disease, and I didn't even know what a balanced meal looked like—nor did I care.

During my third year in graduate school, I had my cholesterol checked for the first time. My years of high-fat dessert eating were evident in the reading of 226. I was very worried about my health; I was also angry that I had to make some changes or risk the health consequences. When I was finished feeling sorry for myself, I began reading everything I could find about nutrition. In assessing my diet, it was clear to me that much of it wasn't too bad (very little fried food, cheese, or high-fat meat) and that the largest source of fat and saturated fat in my diet was sweets. The task of changing my dessert habits was a serious challenge. Undaunted, I made a science out of combing magazine racks and cookbook shelves in search of satisfying dessert recipes that would not be harmful to my health. The search ended in frustration.

Fat-Free Desserts is the product of a personal mission that was sparked by this frustration, a serious concern about my health, and my uncompromising sweet tooth. I now recognize that the bad news about my cholesterol was a critical incident in my life that inspired me not only to take responsibility for my health but also to choose to work in the field of health psychology, the field of psychology that is dedicated to the science and practice of disease prevention and health promotion. The dessert recipes I have created are different from those that have been published in other cookbooks, and they continue to be a satisfying and regular part of my healthy diet. With a cholesterol level that has been safely under 200 for over five years, I am delighted to share my collection of recipes.

2

Baking Without Fat

♦

Taste, Temperature, and Time

The recipes in this cookbook are the result of five years of experimenting, during which time I developed three principles or techniques that I use to create rich-tasting fat-free desserts. Try using these techniques to modify your own favorite recipes. But be persistent—it sometimes takes some tinkering to successfully transform a recipe!

Taste: While your body doesn't care whether you eat plain ol' sugar or other simple, "natural" sugars, your taste buds do. Your taste buds also know when you try to skimp on the amount of sugar in a recipe, and they immediately notify your brain of the attempted deception. Low-sugar or "naturally" sweetened desserts are wasted calories if they aren't satisfying.

In the process of working to develop satisfying but fat-free dessert recipes, I quickly learned that sugar, brown sugar, and powdered sugar give desserts a taste and texture that can't be matched by using sweeteners like honey or fruit juice concentrate. I found that refined sugars, not oils, were essential to delicious, rich-tasting desserts.

But oils do play an important role in making desserts moist.

Hence, I had to find acceptable replacement ingredients that would provide the needed moisture. Instead of oils, my recipes contain ingredients such as plain nonfat yogurt, light corn syrup, skim milk, nonfat buttermilk, chocolate syrup, and fruit juices to moisten the dry ingredients. I never add water because water adds nothing to the taste.

Temperature and Time: Although there are many different types of ingredients that can provide moisture without adding fat, simply finding a substitution is not enough. Oils help keep baked goods moist because the oil does not evaporate during baking. Unlike fat, the liquid in the ingredients used to replace fat does evaporate, so I had to further modify the recipes to make them work. My first experiments baking without fat usually resulted in desserts that were dry around the edges. When I tried decreasing the baking time to prevent the dry edges, the middle section was undercooked.

The temperature and time techniques go hand-in-hand, and they represent the solution to the evaporation problem. By reducing the oven temperature 25°–50° (relative to baking temperatures for most recipes made with fat) and increasing the baking time by 5–10 minutes, the desserts bake more slowly and evenly. It is very important to keep fat-free desserts stored in airtight containers or covered in foil as soon as they are completely cool in order to keep them moist.

Ingredients

Flour: While all of these recipes call for all-purpose white flour, I actually prefer the taste and texture of whole-wheat flour in some of the breads, muffins, and cakes. If you want to try using whole-wheat flour, you will probably need to add extra baking powder or baking soda. Whole-wheat pastry flour is also a good product to use when baking. It contains the fiber and nutrients of whole-wheat flour, but because it is ground more finely, it has a texture similar to white flour.

When measuring flour, do not pack it into the measuring cup. Lightly spoon it into the cup and level it off.

Baking powder: Baking powder has an expiration date printed on the package for a reason. Check the date and invest in a new package if necessary!

Brown sugar: Unless the recipe specifies the use of dark brown sugar, I recommend using light brown sugar. Always pack brown sugar when measuring.

Powdered sugar: I always use 10x powdered sugar because I prefer the texture. When measuring, gently pack the sugar.

Unsweetened cocoa powder: The key ingredient in fat-free chocolate desserts is unsweetened cocoa powder, which is very low in fat. In contrast, chocolate baking squares and chocolate chips are very high in fat.

Vanilla: Always use real vanilla extract. It is more expensive than imitation vanilla flavor, but it's worth it.

Fat-free egg substitute: It is the yolk in an egg that contains the fat and cholesterol. Most fat-free egg substitute products consist mostly of egg whites and work quite well in baked goods. I like using these products, found in the frozen food or dairy section, because they are convenient and easy to use. If you prefer, you can use two egg whites for each one-fourth cup of fat-free egg substitute.

Fat-free margarine: I use small amounts of fat-free margarine (packaged in tubs) to flavor some of my recipes. However, it cannot be used as an equivalent substitute for regular butter in your recipes and cannot be used for frying or sautéing.

Yogurt cream cheese: In addition to replacing the oil in some recipes, nonfat plain yogurt can be used to make fat-free cream cheese. I tried making cheesecake with packaged fat-free cream cheese but didn't like the texture. For a smooth, creamy texture, follow these instructions to make your own yogurt cream cheese. After yogurt is drained for about twenty-four hours, it becomes very thick and can be used like cream cheese in recipes. To drain yogurt, you will need a funnel (two funnels if you are draining thirty-two ounces of yogurt), a coffee filter, and a tall (12–16 ounce) drinking glass. You can buy funnels that are made specifically for draining yogurt, but the funnels in the automotive section of your local discount department store are cheaper and work just fine. The instructions for draining yogurt are as follows:

1. Place the funnel over the drinking glass. Line the funnel with a coffee filter.
2. Spoon 16 ounces or less of plain nonfat yogurt into the coffee filter. Refrigerate for about 24 hours.

Coconut and nuts: Some of the recipes in this cookbook contain small quantities of chopped nuts and coconut, which are high-fat ingredients. (Coconut is particularly high in saturated fat.) In order for the desserts to have less than one-half gram of fat per serving, such ingredients must be kept to a minimum. However, you can add a little extra and still have a very low-fat dessert. But be careful—it's easy to add a lot of fat by adding too much of these ingredients. Use them in moderation, and use the following chart to see what the addition of nuts and coconut will add to the fat and calorie content per serving.

NUTS AND COCONUT: ADDED FAT AND CALORIES

(Grams of fat per serving,
Calories per serving)

		14 servings	10 servings	8 servings
Coconut	⅓ cup	.6g, 8 cal	.8g, 11 cal	1g, 14 cal
(flaked)	¼ cup	.4g, 6 cal	.6g, 8 cal	.8g, 11 cal
	1 tablespoon	.1g, 1 cal	.2g, 2 cal	.2g, 3 cal
Pecans	⅓ cup	2g, 21 cal	2.8g, 29 cal	3.5g, 36 cal
(chopped)	¼ cup	1.5g, 16 cal	2.1g, 22 cal	2.6g, 27 cal
	1 tablespoon	.4g, 4 cal	.5g, 5 cal	.7g, 7 cal
Walnuts	⅓ cup	1.9g, 20 cal	2.6g, 28 cal	3.3g, 35 cal
(chopped)	¼ cup	1.4g, 15 cal	2g, 21 cal	2.5g, 26 cal
	1 tablespoon	.4g, 4 cal	.5g, 5 cal	.6g, 7 cal
Almonds	⅓ cup	2.2g, 24 cal	3.1g, 33 cal	3.8g, 42 cal
(chopped)	¼ cup	1.7g, 18 cal	2.3g, 25 cal	2.9g, 32 cal
	1 tablespoon	.4g, 4 cal	.6g, 6 cal	.7g, 8 cal

To toast nuts or coconut, preheat oven to 350°F. Spread chopped nuts or flaked coconut in an ungreased shallow baking pan. Bake 5 to 10 minutes, stirring frequently, until evenly browned. Watch closely—they burn easily!

3

Cookies, Brownies, and Bars

♠

FUDGE CRINKLE COOKIES

Soft, rich, fudgy, and covered in powdered sugar, these classic cookies taste incredible, look festive, and are surprisingly easy to make. They're perfect for a special occasion, but once you've tried them, you'll find lots of reasons for special occasions!

ABOUT 36 COOKIES; 18 SERVINGS
2 COOKIES PER SERVING

Butter-flavored cooking spray
¼ cup fat-free margarine
2 cups sugar
2 teaspoons vanilla extract
¾ cup fat-free egg substitute
   or 6 egg whites
2 cups flour

¾ cup unsweetened cocoa
   powder
2 teaspoons baking powder
¼ teaspoon salt
1 cup powdered sugar to coat
   cookies

Preheat oven to 325°F. Spray a cookie sheet with cooking spray and wipe with a paper towel to absorb the excess.

Combine margarine, sugar, vanilla, and egg substitute in a large bowl and mix well. In a medium-sized bowl, mix together flour, cocoa, baking powder, and salt. Add flour mixture to the mixture in the large bowl and mix well.

Drop spoonfuls of dough (1–1½ tablespoons each) into powdered sugar and cover completely. Place cookies on cookie sheet. Bake for 10 minutes. Cool for 1 minute before removing from sheet.

NUTRITIONAL INFORMATION PER SERVING			
Calories	164		
Protein	3 g	Dietary fiber	1.5 g
Carbohydrate	37 g	Cholesterol	0 mg
Fat	less than .5 g	Sodium	66 mg
% Calories from fat	3%		

TOUCH-OF-PEANUT-BUTTER COOKIES

It's amazing how much flavor is packed into two tablespoons of peanut butter. My husband likes these better than traditional, full-strength peanut butter cookies!

ABOUT 60 COOKIES; 30 SERVINGS
2 LARGE COOKIES PER SERVING

Butter-flavored cooking spray
¼ cup fat-free margarine
¼ cup pure maple syrup
2 tablespoons reduced-fat
  peanut butter
1½ cups light brown sugar

2 teaspoons vanilla extract
¼ cup fat-free egg substitute
  or 2 egg whites
2 cups flour
1 teaspoon baking soda
½ teaspoon salt

Preheat oven to 325°F. Spray a cookie sheet with cooking spray and wipe with a paper towel to absorb the excess. Combine margarine, maple syrup, peanut butter, brown sugar, vanilla, and egg substitute in a large bowl and mix well. In a medium-sized bowl, mix together flour, baking soda, and salt. Add the flour mixture to the peanut butter mixture and mix well.

Drop spoonfuls of dough (½–1 tablespoon each) onto cookie sheet. Bake for 12 minutes. Cool for 3 minutes on the cookie sheet before removing.

NUTRITIONAL INFORMATION PER SERVING			
Calories	86		
Protein	1g	Dietary fiber	less than .5 g
Carbohydrate	19 g	Cholesterol	0 mg
Fat	less than .5 g	Sodium	91 mg
% Calories from fat	5%		

LEMON COCONUT COOKIES

ABOUT 42 COOKIES; 21 SERVINGS

2 LARGE COOKIES PER SERVING

Butter-flavored cooking spray
½ cup lemonade concentrate, thawed
1½ cups sugar
1 teaspoon vanilla extract
½ teaspoon coconut extract
¼ cup fat-free egg substitute or 2 egg
    whites
2 cups flour
1 teaspoon baking soda
¾ teaspoon salt
¼ cup flaked coconut

Preheat oven to 325°F. Spray a cookie sheet with cooking spray and wipe with a paper towel to absorb the excess. Combine lemonade concentrate, sugar, vanilla, coconut extract, and egg substitute in a large bowl and mix well. In a medium-sized bowl, mix together flour, baking soda, and salt. Add dry mixture to lemonade mixture and mix well. Add coconut and mix well.

Drop spoonfuls of dough (about 1 tablespoon each) onto cookie sheet. Bake for 14 minutes. Cool for 3 minutes on the cookie sheet before removing.

NUTRITIONAL INFORMATION PER SERVING			
Calories	118		
Protein	1.5 g	Dietary fiber	.5 g
Carbohydrate	27	Cholesterol	0 mg
Fat	less than .5 g	Sodium	141 mg
% Calories from fat	3%		

FRUIT-IN-THE-MIDDLE COOKIES
♠

Use several different types of jam or preserves for a variety of tasty cookies.

ABOUT 36 COOKIES; 18 SERVINGS
2 LARGE COOKIES PER SERVING

Butter-flavored cooking spray
2⅔ cups flour
½ teaspoon baking powder
¼ teaspoon cinnamon
½ teaspoon salt
8 ounces nonfat plain yogurt,
   drained (see Index)

1½ cups sugar
3 tablespoons light corn syrup
2 teaspoons vanilla extract
¼ cup fat-free egg substitute
   or 2 egg whites
¾–1 cup jam or preserves

Preheat oven to 325°F. Spray a cookie sheet with cooking spray and wipe with a paper towel to absorb the excess. In a medium-sized bowl, combine flour, baking powder, cinnamon, and salt and mix well. In a large bowl, combine drained yogurt, sugar, corn syrup, vanilla, and egg substitute and mix well. Add dry mixture to wet mixture and mix well.

Drop spoonfuls of dough (1–1½ tablespoons each) onto cookie sheet. Make a shallow indentation in the center of each cookie. Fill each with 1–1½ teaspoons jam or preserves. Bake for 18–20 minutes. Cool for 3 minutes before removing from sheet.

NUTRITIONAL INFORMATION PER SERVING			
Calories	187		
Protein	3 g	Dietary fiber	.5 g
Carbohydrate	44 g	Cholesterol	0 mg
Fat	less than .5 g	Sodium	74 mg
% Calories from fat	1%		

CINNAMON SUGAR COOKIES

ABOUT 40 COOKIES; 20 SERVINGS
2 LARGE COOKIES PER SERVING

Butter-flavored cooking spray
¼ cup fat-free margarine
¼ cup light corn syrup
1½ cups sugar
1 tablespoon vanilla extract
¼ cup fat-free egg substitute
  or 2 egg whites

2 cups flour
1 teaspoon baking soda
½ teaspoon salt
1 cup sugar
1–2 teaspoons cinnamon
  (optional)

Preheat oven to 325°F. Spray a cookie sheet with cooking spray and wipe with a paper towel to absorb the excess. Combine margarine, corn syrup, 1½ cups sugar, vanilla, and egg substitute in a large bowl and mix well. In a medium-sized bowl, combine flour, baking soda, and salt and mix well. Add dry mixture to wet mixture and mix well. In a medium-sized bowl, mix together 1 cup sugar and cinnamon.

Drop spoonfuls of dough (about 1–1½ tablespoons each) into cinnamon sugar to cover. Place cookies on the cookie sheet. Bake for 14 minutes. Cool for 3 minutes on the sheet before removing.

NUTRITIONAL INFORMATION PER SERVING			
Calories	134		
Protein	1.5 g	Dietary fiber	less than .5 g
Carbohydrate	32 g	Cholesterol	0 mg
Fat	less than .5 g	Sodium	142 mg
% Calories from fat	1%		

No-Bake Sugar Cookies

My taste-testing panel loved these cookies, but no one was able to identify the key ingredient—pretzels! The sweet-salty combination makes them a very special treat.

ABOUT 32 COOKIES; 16 SERVINGS
2 LARGE COOKIES PER SERVING

12-ounce bag pretzels
¼ cup fat-free margarine
¼ cup plus 1½ tablespoons plain nonfat
  yogurt
3½ cups powdered sugar
1 teaspoon vanilla extract

Use a food processor to make crumbs out of pretzels. (Do not use salt from the bottom of the bag of pretzels.) Combine margarine, yogurt, sugar, and vanilla in a large bowl and mix well. Add pretzel crumbs and mix well. Use your hands to shape cookies from dough (1–2 tablespoons each).

NUTRITIONAL INFORMATION PER SERVING			
Calories	190		
Protein	2 g	Dietary fiber	.5 g
Carbohydrate	43 g	Cholesterol	0 mg
Fat	less than .5 g	Sodium	528 mg
% Calories from fat	0%		

ALMOND COOKIES

ABOUT 48 COOKIES; 24 SERVINGS

2 COOKIES PER SERVING

114 fat-free saltines
¼ cup fat-free margarine
½ cup plain nonfat yogurt
2 cups powdered sugar
1 teaspoon vanilla extract
1 teaspoon almond extract
2 tablespoons chopped almonds, toasted
  (see Index)
1 cup powdered sugar to coat cookies

Use a food processor to make crumbs out of crackers. Combine margarine, yogurt, powdered sugar, vanilla, and almond extract in a large bowl and mix well. Add cracker crumbs and almonds and mix well. Use your hands to shape cookies from dough (about 1 tablespoon each). Roll each cookie in powdered sugar until covered.

NUTRITIONAL INFORMATION PER SERVING			
Calories	101		
Protein	1.5 g	Dietary fiber	less than .5 g
Carbohydrate	24 g	Cholesterol	0 mg
Fat	less than .5 g	Sodium	126 mg
% Calories from fat	4%		

Ginger Cookies

ABOUT 24 COOKIES; 12 SERVINGS
2 LARGE COOKIES PER SERVING

Butter-flavored cooking spray
¼ cup fat-free margarine
¼ cup molasses
1 cup sugar
2 teaspoons vanilla extract
¼ cup fat-free egg substitute
    or 2 egg whites

2 cups flour
1 teaspoon baking soda
½ teaspoon salt
1 teaspoon ginger
1 teaspoon cinnamon
1 cup sugar to coat cookies

Preheat oven to 325°F. Spray a cookie sheet with cooking spray and wipe with a paper towel to absorb the excess. Combine the margarine, molasses, 1 cup sugar, vanilla, and egg substitute in a large bowl and mix well. In a medium-sized bowl, mix together flour, baking soda, salt, ginger, and cinnamon. Add flour mixture to molasses mixture and mix well.

Drop spoonfuls of dough (1½–2 tablespoons each) into 1 cup sugar to cover. Place cookies on cookie sheet. Bake for 14 minutes. Cool for 3 minutes on the cookie sheet before removing.

NUTRITIONAL INFORMATION PER SERVING			
Calories	270		
Protein	4 g	Dietary fiber	1 g
Carbohydrate	63 g	Cholesterol	0 mg
Fat	less than .5 g	Sodium	352 mg
% Calories from fat	1%		

OATMEAL RAISIN COOKIES

It is my opinion that salsa, not cookies, should be spicy. However, I realize that many people, like my friend and colleague Hal Currey, like their oatmeal cookies spicy. Hal was kind enough to give me the blend of spices used by his mother, Louise, in her oatmeal cookies. So if you like 'em spicy, add two teaspoons nutmeg, one-half teaspoon clove, and one-half teaspoon allspice to the recipe below.

ABOUT 36 COOKIES; 18 SERVINGS
2 LARGE COOKIES PER SERVING

Butter-flavored cooking spray
¼ cup fat-free margarine
¼ cup light corn syrup
1½ cups light brown sugar
2 teaspoons vanilla extract
¼ cup fat-free egg substitute or 2 egg
   whites
¼ cup skim milk
⅔ cup quick oats
2⅓ cups flour
½ teaspoon baking soda
½ teaspoon salt
2 teaspoons cinnamon
2 cups raisins

Preheat oven to 325°F. Spray a cookie sheet with cooking spray and wipe with a paper towel to absorb the excess. Combine margarine, corn syrup, brown sugar, vanilla, egg substitute, and milk in a large bowl and mix well. In a medium-sized bowl, mix together oats, flour, baking soda, salt, and cinnamon. Add oats mixture to the mixture in the large bowl and mix well. Stir in raisins.

Drop spoonfuls of dough (1½–2 tablespoons each) onto cookie sheet and bake for 15 minutes. Cool for 3 minutes on the cookie sheet before removing.

NUTRITIONAL INFORMATION PER SERVING			
Calories	212		
Protein	3.5 g	Dietary fiber	1 g
Carbohydrate	49 g	Cholesterol	0 mg
Fat	less than .5 g	Sodium	133 mg
% Calories from fat	2%		

FUDGE BROWNIES

*Developing a truly delicious brownie recipe without using whole
eggs, butter, oil, or chocolate chips was a serious challenge. But no
dessert cookbook would be complete without brownies! These are
tasty plain, but for complete brownie decadence, make them with
one of the five toppings that follow.*

15 SERVINGS

Butter-flavored cooking spray   ⅓ *cup chocolate syrup*
Flour to coat pan   ⅓ *cup light corn syrup*
1½ *cups flour*   ⅔ *cup plain nonfat yogurt*
½ *cup unsweetened cocoa*   ¼ *cup fat-free egg substitute*
   powder   *or 2 egg whites*
1½ *cups sugar*   ¼ *cup skim milk*
⅛ *teaspoon baking powder*   2 *teaspoons vanilla extract*
½ *teaspoon salt*

Preheat oven to 300°F. Spray a 13″ × 9″ pan with cooking spray
and wipe with a paper towel to absorb the excess. Dust pan with
flour and shake out the excess.

In a large bowl, combine 1½ cups flour, cocoa, sugar, baking
powder, and salt. To the dry mixture, add remaining ingredients
and mix well. Pour batter into pan evenly. Bake for 30 minutes.
Cool before cutting into bars.

NUTRITIONAL INFORMATION PER SERVING			
Calories	185		
Protein	3 g	Dietary fiber	1.2 g
Carbohydrate	42 g	Cholesterol	0 mg
Fat	less than .5 g	Sodium	96 mg
% Calories from fat	2%		

DOUBLE CHOCOLATE BROWNIES

Fudge Brownies (see Index)
2 cups powdered sugar
1½ tablespoons unsweetened
  cocoa powder

Pinch of salt
¼ cup skim milk
1 teaspoon vanilla extract

Make Fudge Brownies. In a medium-sized bowl, mix together remaining ingredients. Spread icing evenly over warm brownies.

NUTRITIONAL INFORMATION PER SERVING			
Calories	252		
Protein	3.5 g	Dietary fiber	1.3 g
Carbohydrate	59 g	Cholesterol	0 mg
Fat	less than .5 g	Sodium	99 mg
% Calories from fat	2%		

MOCHA BROWNIES

Fudge Brownies (see Index)
¼ cup skim milk, warmed to
  just before boiling
2 tablespoons instant coffee
  granules

2 cups powdered sugar
1 teaspoon vanilla extract
Pinch of salt

Make Fudge Brownies. In a medium-sized bowl, mix together remaining ingredients. Spread icing evenly over warm brownies.

NUTRITIONAL INFORMATION PER SERVING			
Calories	251		
Protein	3.5 g	Dietary fiber	1.2 g
Carbohydrate	59 g	Cholesterol	0 mg
Fat	less than .5 g	Sodium	106 mg
% Calories from fat	2%		

RASPBERRY BROWNIES

Fudge Brownies (see Index)
8 ounces plain nonfat yogurt,
* drained (see Index)*
½ cup seedless raspberry jam

1½ cups powdered sugar
1 tablespoon unsweetened
* cocoa powder*
Pinch of salt

Make Fudge Brownies. In a medium-sized bowl, combine remaining ingredients and mix well. Spread icing evenly over warm brownies.

NUTRITIONAL INFORMATION PER SERVING			
Calories	251		
Protein	3.5 g	Dietary fiber	1.2 g
Carbohydrate	59 g	Cholesterol	0 mg
Fat	less than .5 g	Sodium	106 mg
% Calories from fat	2%		

MINT BROWNIES

Fudge Brownies (see Index)
2 cups powdered sugar
Pinch of salt
¼ cup skim milk

¼ teaspoon mint extract
3 drops green food color
* (optional)*

Make Fudge Brownies. In a medium-sized bowl, mix together remaining ingredients. Spread icing evenly over warm brownies.

NUTRITIONAL INFORMATION PER SERVING			
Calories	248		
Protein	3.5 g	Dietary fiber	1.2 g
Carbohydrate	58 g	Cholesterol	0 mg
Fat	less than .5 g	Sodium	106 mg
% Calories from fat	2%		

Oatmeal Raisin Cookies (recipe on pages 22–23) ▶

CARAMEL BROWNIES

Fudge Brownies (see Index)
½ cup skim milk
1 cup dark brown sugar
⅛ teaspoon salt
1 tablespoon fat-free margarine
1 teaspoon vanilla extract
¾ cup powdered sugar

Make Fudge Brownies. In a small sauce pan, combine milk, brown sugar, and salt. Cook over low heat until sugar is melted. Bring to a hard boil over medium heat. Remove from heat and add margarine and vanilla. Stir until mixed well. Cool.

Pour mixture into a medium-sized bowl and beat for 3 minutes. Add powdered sugar and mix well. Spread icing evenly over brownies.

NUTRITIONAL INFORMATION PER SERVING			
Calories	267		
Protein	3.5 g	Dietary fiber	1 g
Carbohydrate	63 g	Cholesterol	0 mg
Fat	less than .5 g	Sodium	116 mg
% Calories from fat	1%		

BUTTERSCOTCH OAT BARS

12 SERVINGS

Butter-flavored cooking spray
3 cups flour
¼ cup quick oats
1 teaspoon baking soda
1 teaspoon salt
1½ cups light brown sugar

¼ cup fat-free margarine
2 teaspoons vanilla extract
¼ cup skim milk
1 cup fat-free butterscotch
*   sundae topping*
3 tablespoons flour

Preheat oven to 325°F. Spray a 13″ X 9″ pan with cooking spray and wipe with a paper towel to absorb excess.

In a large bowl, combine 3 cups flour, oats, baking soda, and salt and mix well. Add brown sugar, margarine, vanilla, and milk. Mix until crumbly and evenly moistened. Remove 1 cup of crumb mixture and reserve. Press the rest of the crumb mixture evenly into pan.

In a small bowl, combine butterscotch topping and 3 tablespoons flour and mix well. Spread butterscotch mixture evenly over crumb mixture in pan. Sprinkle reserved crumbs over butterscotch mixture. Bake for 20 minutes. Cool completely. Cut into bars.

NUTRITIONAL INFORMATION PER SERVING			
Calories	310		
Protein	4 g	Dietary fiber	1 g
Carbohydrate	72 g	Cholesterol	0 mg
Fat	less than .5 g	Sodium	374 mg
% Calories from fat	1%		

MOCHA CHEWS

These bars have the consistency of brownies and are flavored with a wonderful blend of coffee, cocoa, dark brown sugar, and a hint of cinnamon. You can vary the flavor by choosing different flavors of creamer (found in your supermarket's dairy section)— one of my favorites is hazelnut.

12 SERVINGS

BARS
Butter-flavored cooking spray
Flour to coat pan
1½ cups flour
¼ cup unsweetened cocoa powder
¾ cup powdered sugar
⅛ teaspoon baking powder
½ teaspoon salt
½ teaspoon cinnamon
1½ cups dark brown sugar
½ cup cold coffee
2 tablespoons fat-free margarine
¼ cup fat-free egg substitute or 2 egg
    whites
¼ cup fat-free liquid creamer, flavored
1 teaspoon vanilla extract

GLAZE
½ cup powdered sugar
1 tablespoon cold coffee
Pinch of salt

Preheat oven to 300°F. Spray a 13″ × 9 ″ pan with cooking spray and wipe with a paper towel to absorb the excess. Dust pan thoroughly with flour and shake out the excess.

In a small bowl, combine 1½ cups flour, cocoa, powdered sugar, baking powder, salt, and cinnamon and mix well. In a large bowl, combine remaining ingredients and mix well. Add dry mixture to wet mixture and mix well. Pour batter into pan evenly. Bake for 30 minutes. Cool completely.

Combine glaze ingredients and mix well. Drizzle glaze over top. Cut into bars.

NUTRITIONAL INFORMATION PER SERVING			
Calories	229		
Protein	2.5 g	Dietary fiber	1 g
Carbohydrate	54 g	Cholesterol	0 mg
Fat	less than .5 g	Sodium	138 mg
% Calories from fat	1%		

CHOCOLATE CHEESECAKE BARS

These bars are smooth, rich, and very chocolaty. If you'd like, add one-quarter cup chopped walnuts or pecans to the crust mixture. See Index for chart that tells what this will add to the fat and calorie content per serving.

9 SERVINGS

CRUST	TOPPING
Butter-flavored cooking spray	16 ounces plain nonfat
¼ cup fat-free margarine	yogurt, drained (see Index)
½ cup light brown sugar	¼ cup fat-free egg substitute
1 cup flour	or 2 egg whites
⅛ teaspoon salt	¾ cup sugar
	⅓ cup unsweetened cocoa
	powder
	¼ cup skim milk
	¼ teaspoon vanilla extract
	¼ teaspoon salt

Preheat oven to 325°F. Spray an 8-inch square pan with cooking spray and wipe with a paper towel to absorb the excess. In a medium-sized bowl, combine crust ingredients and mix well. Press crust dough into the bottom of pan.

In a medium-sized bowl, combine topping ingredients and mix well. Pour the topping over the crust. Bake for 25–30 minutes. Cool completely before cutting into bars and serving.

NUTRITIONAL INFORMATION PER SERVING			
Calories	202		
Protein	6 g	Dietary fiber	1 g
Carbohydrate	44 g	Cholesterol	1 mg
Fat	less than .5 g	Sodium	170 mg
% Calories from fat	2%		

CHEWY DATE BARS

If you'd like, try adding some chopped pecans to these tasty, chewy bars. See the Index for chart that tells what it would add to the fat and calorie content per serving.

12 SERVINGS

Butter-flavored cooking spray
Flour to coat pan
1 cup flour
½ teaspoon baking powder
¼ teaspoon salt
½ teaspoon cinnamon
1 cup light brown sugar

¾ cup fat-free egg substitute
  or 6 egg whites
2 teaspoons vanilla extract
2 8-ounce packages pitted,
  chopped dates
¼ cup powdered sugar

Preheat oven to 300°F. Spray a 13″ × 9″ pan with cooking spray and wipe with a paper towel to spread cooking spray and absorb the excess. Dust pan with flour and shake out the excess.

In a small bowl, combine 1 cup flour, baking powder, salt, and cinnamon and mix well. In a large bowl, combine brown sugar, egg substitute, and vanilla and mix well. Add dry mixture to wet mixture and mix well. Stir in dates. Spoon batter into pan and spread evenly. Bake for 30 minutes.

Cool completely. Cut into bars. Use a fine strainer to dust bars with powdered sugar.

NUTRITIONAL INFORMATION PER SERVING			
Calories	230		
Protein	3 g	Dietary fiber	3.5 g
Carbohydrate	57 g	Cholesterol	0 mg
Fat	less than .5 g	Sodium	74 mg
% Calories from fat	1%		

CHOCOLATE CARAMEL BARS

15 SERVINGS

BARS
Butter-flavored cooking spray
3 cups flour
¼ cup quick oats
1 teaspoon baking soda
1 teaspoon salt
1½ cups light brown sugar
¼ cup fat-free margarine
2 teaspoons vanilla extract
¼ cup skim milk
1 cup fat-free caramel sundae topping
3 tablespoons flour

ICING
1½ cups powdered sugar
3½ tablespoons unsweetened cocoa powder
⅛ teaspoon salt
4–5 tablespoons skim milk
½ teaspoon vanilla extract

Preheat oven to 325°F. Spray a 13″ × 9″ pan with cooking spray and wipe with a paper towel to absorb the excess. In a large bowl, combine 3 cups flour, oats, baking soda, and salt and mix well. Add brown sugar, margarine, vanilla, and milk. Mix until crumbly and evenly moistened. Remove 1 cup of crumb mixture and reserve. Press the rest of the crumb mixture evenly into pan.

In a small bowl, combine caramel topping and 3 tablespoons flour and mix well. Spread caramel mixture evenly over crumbs in pan. Sprinkle reserved crumbs over caramel sauce mixture. Bake for 20 minutes. Cool completely.

   Combine icing ingredients in a medium-sized bowl and mix well. Drizzle icing evenly over top. Cut into bars.

NUTRITIONAL INFORMATION PER SERVING			
Calories	302		
Protein	3.5 g	Dietary fiber	1 g
Carbohydrate	70 g	Cholesterol	0 mg
Fat	less than .5 g	Sodium	319 mg
% Calories from fat	1%		

LEMON CUSTARD BARS

These bars have a cookie-like crust; a creamy, tangy custard topping; and less than 200 calories per serving!

9 SERVINGS

CRUST
Butter-flavored cooking spray
¼ *cup fat-free margarine*
1 *cup powdered sugar*
1 *cup flour*
⅛ *teaspoon salt*
1 *teaspoon vanilla extract*

TOPPING
½ *cup fat-free egg substitute or 4 egg whites*
1 *cup sugar*
2 *tablespoons flour*
¼ *teaspoon baking powder*
⅛ *teaspoon salt*
1 *teaspoon finely grated lemon rind*
3 *tablespoons lemon juice*
Powdered sugar to dust bars (optional)

Preheat oven to 325°F. Spray an 8-inch square pan with cooking spray and wipe with a paper towel to absorb the excess. In a medium-sized bowl, combine crust ingredients and mix well. Spread crust dough over the bottom of pan.

In a small bowl, combine topping ingredients and mix well. Pour the topping over the crust. Bake for 27–30 minutes. Cool completely before cutting into bars and serving. Dust bars with powdered sugar when cool, if desired.

NUTRITIONAL INFORMATION PER SERVING			
Calories	197		
Protein	3 g	Dietary fiber	.5 g
Carbohydrate	47 g	Cholesterol	0 mg
Fat	less than .5 g	Sodium	119 mg
% Calories from fat	1%		

RASPBERRY COCONUT CREAM BARS

One person on my taste-testing panel said that these bars taste like they're full of calories. They are actually surprisingly low in calories—only 173 per serving!

9 SERVINGS

CRUST

Butter-flavored cooking spray
25 fat-free wheat crackers
2 reduced-fat vanilla
  sandwich cookies
1 tablespoon fat-free
  margarine
¼ cup seedless raspberry jam
¾ cup powdered sugar

TOPPING

8 ounces plain nonfat yogurt,
  drained (see Index)
¼ teaspoon vanilla extract
⅛ teaspoon coconut extract
Pinch of salt
1 cup powdered sugar
1 tablespoon flaked coconut,
  toasted (see Index)

Spray an 8-inch square pan with cooking spray and wipe with a paper towel. Blend crackers and cookies in a food processor to make crumbs. In a medium-sized bowl, combine margarine, jam, and ¾ cup powdered sugar. Stir crumbs into jam mixture and mix well. Press mixture into the bottom of pan.

    In a medium-sized bowl, combine first five topping ingredients and mix well. Pour topping over crust. Sprinkle with coconut. Chill several hours before cutting into bars and serving.

NUTRITIONAL INFORMATION PER SERVING			
Calories	173		
Protein	2.5 g	Dietary fiber	less than 1 g
Carbohydrate	40 g	Cholesterol	0 mg
Fat	less than .5 g	Sodium	145 mg
% Calories from fat	2%		

Fudge Brownies (recipe on page 24) ▶

BUTTERSCOTCH FUDGE SWIRL BARS

12 SERVINGS

Butter-flavored cooking spray
Flour to coat pan
2 cups flour
½ cup powdered sugar
2 cups sugar
¼ teaspoon baking powder
1 teaspoon salt
1 cup plain nonfat yogurt

½ cup fat-free egg substitute
 or 4 egg whites
2 teaspoons vanilla extract
3 tablespoons unsweetened
 cocoa powder
1 tablespoon skim milk
1 cup fat-free butterscotch
 sundae topping

Preheat oven to 325°F. Spray a 13″ × 9″ pan with cooking spray and wipe with a paper towel to absorb the excess. Dust pan thoroughly with flour and shake out the excess.

In a small bowl, combine flour, powdered sugar, sugar, baking powder, and salt and mix well. In a large bowl, combine yogurt, egg substitute, and vanilla and mix well. Add dry mixture to wet mixture and mix well. Remove 1 cup of batter and reserve in a small bowl. Add cocoa and milk to the reserved 1 cup batter in the *small* bowl and mix well. Add butterscotch sauce to the batter in the *large* bowl and mix well.

Pour butterscotch batter into pan evenly. Spoon chocolate batter over butterscotch batter in stripes. Use a fork to swirl the batter. Bake 30–40 minutes. Cool completely. Cut into bars.

NUTRITIONAL INFORMATION PER SERVING			
Calories	333		
Protein	4.5 g	Dietary fiber	1 g
Carbohydrate	78 g	Cholesterol	0 mg
Fat	less than .5 g	Sodium	286 mg
% Calories from fat	1%		

4

Cakes

Chocolate Fudge Layer Cake

15 SERVINGS

CAKE
Butter-flavored cooking spray
2 cups flour
½ cup powdered sugar
4 tablespoons unsweetened cocoa powder
1½ teaspoons baking powder
¾ teaspoon salt
1 cup sugar
½ cup fat-free egg substitute or 4 egg
  whites
¾ cup skim milk
1 cup chocolate syrup
2 teaspoons vanilla extract

ICING
3 cups powdered sugar
4 tablespoons unsweetened cocoa powder
Pinch of salt
½ teaspoon vanilla extract
1 11½-ounce jar fat-free hot fudge topping
  (about 1 cup)

Preheat oven to 325°F. Spray three 8½-inch round cake pans with cooking spray and wipe with a paper towel to absorb the excess.

In a medium-sized bowl, combine flour, powdered sugar, cocoa, baking powder, and salt and mix well. In a large bowl, combine sugar, egg substitute, milk, chocolate syrup, and vanilla and mix well. Add the dry mixture to the wet mixture and mix well. Spoon batter into the three pans equally. Bake for 23 minutes. Allow cakes to cool 5 minutes before removing from pans. Remove cakes from pans and cool completely.

In a large bowl, combine icing ingredients and mix well. Icing should be thick but spreadable. Assemble cake by covering two layers of cake with icing. Stack these iced layers and top them with the plain cake layer. Spread the rest of the icing over the top and sides of cake. Store in an airtight container to keep the cake moist.

NUTRITIONAL INFORMATION PER SERVING			
Calories	336		
Protein	5 g	Dietary fiber	1.3 g
Carbohydrate	80 g	Cholesterol	0 mg
Fat	less than .5 g	Sodium	169 mg
% Calories from fat	1%		

CHOCOLATE CARAMEL CAKE

This rich dessert is reminiscent of those delicious chocolate-covered caramel-and-pecan candies. This is one of my favorites. If you'd like, add more pecans. See the Index for chart that tells what this will add to the fat and calorie content per serving.

15 SERVINGS

CARAMEL TOPPING
1 cup dark brown sugar
½ cup skim milk
⅛ teaspoon salt
1 tablespoon fat-free margarine
1 teaspoon vanilla extract
1 teaspoon finely chopped pecans

CAKE
Butter-flavored cooking spray
1 cup sugar
1 cup light brown sugar
2 cups flour
½ teaspoon baking powder
½ teaspoon salt
⅓ cup plain nonfat yogurt
1 cup nonfat buttermilk
¼ cup fat-free egg substitute or 2 egg whites
1 teaspoon vanilla extract

ICING
2 cups powdered sugar
3 tablespoons unsweetened cocoa powder
⅛ teaspoon salt
⅓ cup skim milk
½ teaspoon vanilla extract

To make caramel topping, combine the dark brown sugar, milk, and salt in a medium-sized saucepan. Cook over low heat until sugar is melted, stirring continuously. Bring to a hard boil over medium heat, stirring continuously. Mixture will begin to rise. Simmer, stirring continuously, for about 2 minutes. Remove pan from heat and add margarine, stirring until it is dissolved. Add vanilla and pecans and stir. Set topping aside to cool.

Preheat oven to 325°F. Spray a 13″ × 9″ pan with cooking spray and wipe with a paper towel to spread the cooking spray evenly and absorb the excess. In a large bowl, combine sugar, light brown sugar, flour, baking powder, and salt and mix well. Add yogurt and mix with a fork until mixture is evenly moistened and crumblike. Remove and reserve ½ cup of the crumb mixture. Add buttermilk, egg substitute, and vanilla to the crumb mixture in the large bowl and mix well.

Pour batter into pan. Bake for 15 minutes. Remove cake from oven and drizzle cooled caramel topping evenly over the top. Sprinkle the reserved crumb mixture over the caramel topping. Return cake to oven and bake for an additional 20 minutes. Remove cake from oven.

Combine icing ingredients and mix well. Drizzle icing evenly over warm cake.

NUTRITIONAL INFORMATION PER SERVING			
Calories	308		
Protein	3.5 g	Dietary fiber	less than 1 g
Carbohydrate	73 g	Cholesterol	less than 1 mg
Fat	less than .5 g	Sodium	159 mg
% Calories from fat	1%		

BLACK FOREST CAKE

14 SERVINGS

CAKE
Butter-flavored cooking spray
1¾ cups flour
1⅔ cups powdered sugar
5 tablespoons unsweetened cocoa powder
1 teaspoon baking soda
1 teaspoon salt
¼ cup sugar
¼ cup brandy
½ cup egg substitute or 4 egg whites
½ cup skim milk
½ cup chocolate syrup
1 teaspoon vanilla extract

FILLING/TOPPING
1 7.2-ounce box fat-free fluffy white
   frosting mix
½ cup boiling water
1 21-ounce can cherry pie filling

Preheat oven to 325°F. Spray three 8½-inch round cake pans with cooking spray and wipe with a paper towel to absorb the excess.

In a medium-sized bowl, combine flour, powdered sugar, cocoa, baking soda, and salt and mix well. In a large bowl, combine sugar, brandy, egg substitute, milk, chocolate syrup, and vanilla and mix well. Add the dry mixture to the wet mixture and mix well. Spoon batter into the three pans equally. Bake for 20 minutes.

Allow cakes to cool for 5 minutes before removing from pans. Remove cakes from pans and cool completely.

To make topping/filling, in a large bowl, combine frosting mix and boiling water. Beat until mix is melted. Beat on high until mixture is fluffy and stiff peaks form. Fold in cherry pie filling.

Assemble cake by covering two layers of cake with topping/ filling. Stack these layers and top them with the plain cake layer. Cover the top and sides of cake with remaining topping/filling. Refrigerate for several hours before serving.

NUTRITIONAL INFORMATION PER SERVING			
Calories	283		
Protein	4 g	Dietary fiber	1 g
Carbohydrate	64 g	Cholesterol	0 mg
Fat	less than .5 g	Sodium	305 mg
Alcohol	1.4 g		
% Calories from fat	1%		

ROCKY ROAD CAKE

For an extra special treat, stir some chopped pecans into the batter before baking. See Index for chart that tells what this will add to the fat and calorie content per serving.

15 SERVINGS

CAKE
Butter-flavored cooking spray
1½ cups flour
½ teaspoon baking powder
½ teaspoon salt
½ cup unsweetened cocoa powder
2 cups sugar
1 cup fat-free egg substitute or 8 egg
   whites
½ cup skim milk
2 teaspoons vanilla extract
1 10½-ounce bag miniature
   marshmallows

GLAZE
1 cup powdered sugar
Pinch of salt
1 tablespoon unsweetened cocoa powder
2–3 tablespoons skim milk
½ teaspoon vanilla extract

Preheat oven to 325°F. Spray a 13″ × 9″ pan with cooking spray and wipe with a paper towel to spread cooking spray evenly and absorb the excess.

In a medium-sized bowl, combine flour, baking powder, salt, and cocoa and mix well. In a large bowl, combine sugar, egg

substitute, milk, and vanilla and mix well. Add dry mixture to
wet mixture and mix well. Pour batter into pan. Bake for 25
minutes. Remove cake from oven and cover with marshmallows.
Return cake to oven and bake for an additional 5 minutes.

   Combine glaze ingredients and mix well. Drizzle glaze over
warm cake.

NUTRITIONAL INFORMATION PER SERVING			
Calories	269		
Protein	4.5 g	Dietary fiber	1 g
Carbohydrate	63 g	Cholesterol	0 mg
Fat	less than .5 g	Sodium	115 mg
% Calories from fat	2%		

RING OF FUDGE CAKE

*This cake is filled with a beautiful ring of fudge and has an
outer shell of vanilla cake that's covered with a chocolate glaze.*

14 SERVINGS

CAKE
Butter-flavored cooking spray
1¾ *cup sugar*
½ *cup plain nonfat yogurt*
2 *cups powdered sugar*
¼ *cup skim milk*
½ *cup fat-free egg substitute or 4 egg
   whites*
2 *teaspoons vanilla extract*
2¼ *cups flour*
½ *teaspoon baking powder*
1 *teaspoon salt*
⅓ *cup unsweetened cocoa powder*
¼ *cup light corn syrup*

GLAZE
½ *cup powdered sugar*
1½ *tablespoons unsweetened cocoa*
Pinch of salt
1½–2 *tablespoons skim milk*

Preheat oven to 325°F. Spray a Bundt pan thoroughly with
cooking spray and wipe with a paper towel to spread cooking
spray evenly and absorb the excess.

In a large bowl, combine sugar, yogurt, powdered sugar, milk,
egg substitute, and vanilla and mix well. In a medium-sized
bowl, combine flour, baking powder, and salt and mix well. Add

dry mixture to wet mixture and stir well. Remove 2 cups of batter and put in a small bowl. Add cocoa and corn syrup and stir until well mixed.

Spoon all but 1–1½ cups of the plain batter into pan. Spoon fudge batter in a two-inch ring in the center of the plain batter in the pan. Spoon reserved plain batter into the pan to cover the fudge batter ring. Bake for 1 hour and 5 minutes. Allow cake to cool for 10 minutes before removing it from pan.

Combine glaze ingredients. Drizzle glaze over warm cake.

NUTRITIONAL INFORMATION PER SERVING			
Calories	294		
Protein	4 g	Dietary fiber	1 g
Carbohydrate	69 g	Cholesterol	0 mg
Fat	less than .5 g	Sodium	187 mg
% Calories from fat	1%		

QUICK CHOCOLATE TORTE

Fast, attractive, and delicious!

8 SERVINGS

1 fat-free golden loaf or pound cake
½ cup nonfat sour cream
1½ cups powdered sugar
¼ cup unsweetened cocoa powder
½ teaspoon vanilla extract

Slice cake horizontally into thirds. Combine remaining ingredients and mix well. Spread a thin layer of icing between the cake layers and assemble cake. Spread remaining icing over the top and sides of cake.

NUTRITIONAL INFORMATION PER SERVING			
Calories	221		
Protein	4 g	Dietary fiber	1 g
Carbohydrate	52 g	Cholesterol	0 mg
Fat	less than .5 g	Sodium	180 mg
% Calories from fat	1%		

Easy Three-Layer Cake

This dessert has a chocolate layer on the bottom, a cake layer in the middle, and a caramelized layer on top—and it's simple to make! If you'd like, sprinkle a few pecans or almonds over the top before baking. See Index for chart that tells what this will add to the fat and calorie content per serving.

12 SERVINGS

1 cup light brown sugar
½ cup unsweetened cocoa powder
2 cups skim milk
2 cups miniature marshmallows
1 16-ounce boxed white angel food cake
    mix
1⅓ cups skim milk
1 teaspoon vanilla extract

Preheat oven to 325°F. In a medium-sized bowl, combine brown sugar, cocoa, and 2 cups milk and mix well. Pour mixture into a 13″ × 9″ pan. Sprinkle marshmallows evenly over brown sugar mixture in pan.

In a medium-sized bowl, combine cake mix, 1⅓ cups milk, and vanilla and mix well. Pour batter evenly over mixture in pan. Bake for 45 minutes.

Cool before serving. Use a spatula to remove from pan.

NUTRITIONAL INFORMATION PER SERVING			
Calories	285		
Protein	6.5 g	Dietary fiber	1 g
Carbohydrate	64 g	Cholesterol	1 mg
Fat	less than .5 g	Sodium	346 mg
% Calories from fat	1%		

SACHERTORTE

12 SERVINGS

CAKE
Butter-flavored cooking spray
1½ cups flour
¼ teaspoon baking powder
1 teaspoon salt
¼ cup unsweetened cocoa powder
¾ cup powdered sugar
1 cup sugar
¾ cup apricot nectar
1 teaspoon vanilla extract
¼ cup fat-free egg substitute or 2 egg
   whites

TOPPING
½ cup apricot preserves
½ cup powdered sugar
2 tablespoons unsweetened cocoa powder
Pinch of salt
1½ tablespoons skim milk
¼ teaspoon vanilla extract

Preheat oven to 325°F. Spray base of a 10-inch springform pan
with cooking spray and wipe with a paper towel. Cover base of
pan with waxed paper. Attach sides of pan. Use scissors to trim
excess waxed paper. Spray waxed paper and sides of pan with
cooking spray and wipe with a paper towel to spread cooking
spray evenly and absorb the excess.

In a small bowl, combine flour, baking powder, salt, cocoa,
and powdered sugar and mix well. In a large bowl, combine

sugar, apricot nectar, vanilla, and egg substitute and mix well. Add dry mixture to the wet mixture and mix well. Spread batter evenly over bottom of pan.

Bake for 30 minutes. Cool cake for about 10 minutes. Remove sides of pan and slide cake and waxed paper onto a serving plate. Spread apricot preserves over the top and sides of the cake. Cool cake completely.

Combine remaining topping ingredients. Drizzle topping over cake and serve.

NUTRITIONAL INFORMATION PER SERVING			
Calories	230		
Protein	3 g	Dietary fiber	1.4 g
Carbohydrate	54 g	Cholesterol	0 mg
Fat	less than .5 g	Sodium	198 mg
% Calories from fat	2%		

Pumpkin–Cream Cheese Swirl Cake

12 SERVINGS

CAKE
Butter-flavored cooking spray
2 cups flour
2 teaspoons baking powder
1 teaspoon baking soda
¾ teaspoon salt
2 teaspoons cinnamon
1½ cups sugar
1 16-ounce can solid-pack pumpkin
½ cup skim milk
½ cup plain nonfat yogurt
1 teaspoon vanilla extract
¼ teaspoon maple flavor

CREAM CHEESE SWIRL
16 oz. plain nonfat yogurt, drained (see Index)
1 cup sugar
⅛ teaspoon salt
¼ cup fat-free egg substitute or 2 egg whites
½ teaspoon vanilla extract
¼ teaspoon maple flavor

Preheat oven to 325°F. Spray a 13″ × 9″ pan with cooking spray and wipe with a paper towel to spread cooking spray evenly and absorb the excess. In a medium-sized bowl, combine flour, baking powder, baking soda, salt, and cinnamon and mix well. In a large bowl, combine sugar, pumpkin, milk, yogurt, vanilla, and maple flavor and mix well. Add dry mixture to wet mixture and mix well. Spread batter evenly in pan.

In a medium-sized bowl, combine cream cheese swirl ingredients and mix well. Spread cream cheese swirl evenly over batter.

Scoop up about 12 spoonfuls of batter and cream cheese swirl and turn each spoonful over so that there are dots of batter showing. Use a fork to swirl the batter and cream cheese swirl well. Bake for 40 minutes. Cool cake completely.

NUTRITIONAL INFORMATION PER SERVING			
Calories	281		
Protein	6 g	Dietary fiber	1.7 g
Carbohydrate	65 g	Cholesterol	1 mg
Fat	less than .5 g	Sodium	308 mg
% Calories from fat	1%		

SOUR CREAM CAKE

You can create your own unique flavor by varying the flavor of pudding and liqueur you add to this cake. My favorite is a butterscotch pudding–amaretto combination. Have fun experimenting!

12 SERVINGS

CAKE
Butter-flavored cooking spray
Flour to coat pan
1 16-ounce boxed white angel food cake
   mix
1 3–4-ounce box instant pudding mix,
   any flavor
¾ cup nonfat sour cream
⅓ cup light corn syrup
½ cup skim milk
¼ cup fat-free mayonnaise-style salad
   dressing
½ cup fat-free egg substitute or 4 egg
   whites
1 teaspoon vanilla extract
3 tablespoons liqueur, any flavor
1 tablespoon pecans, chopped finely

ICING
1½ cups nonfat sour cream
⅔ cup light brown sugar
1 teaspoon vanilla extract

Preheat oven to 325°F. Spray a 13″ × 9″ pan with cooking spray and wipe with a paper towel to spread cooking spray evenly and absorb the excess. Dust pan with flour and shake out the excess.

In a large bowl, combine the cake mix and pudding mix. Add remaining ingredients except pecans and mix well. Stir in pecans. Pour batter into pan. Bake for 25 minutes.

Combine icing ingredients and mix well. Pour icing over warm cake and spread evenly.

NUTRITIONAL INFORMATION PER SERVING			
Calories	334		
Protein	8 g	Dietary fiber	0 g
Carbohydrate	72 g	Cholesterol	0 mg
Fat	less than .5 g	Sodium	501 mg
Alcohol	1.2 g		
% Calories from fat	1%		

Irish-Coffee Cake

The original recipe for this cake was created by my friend and colleague, Pat O'Neil. I modified it, of course, to make it fat-free. It combines the flavors and the kick that make Irish coffee such a special treat. Pat recommends that you "give the cake a drink or two" by drizzling three-fourths ounce of Irish whiskey over the cake once or twice the day after you make the cake. He also recommends serving it with a scoop of coffee ice cream (low-fat, of course!). See Index for a fat-free coffee ice cream recipe.

12 SERVINGS

CAKE
Butter-flavored cooking spray
½ cup quick oats
2 cups flour
2 teaspoons baking powder
1 teaspoon salt
1 teaspoon cinnamon
¼ teaspoon mace
¼ teaspoon cloves
1½ cups dark brown sugar
½ cup fat-free egg substitute or 4 egg
    whites
1 teaspoon vanilla extract
½ fat-free liquid creamer, Irish creme
    flavor
½ cup very strong cool coffee

GLAZE
½ cup powdered sugar
¼ cup very strong cool coffee
⅓ cup Irish whiskey

Preheat oven to 325°F. Spray a Bundt pan with cooking spray and wipe with a paper towel to absorb the excess.

Process oats in a food processor. In a medium-sized bowl, combine oats, flour, baking powder, salt, cinnamon, mace, and cloves and mix well. In a large bowl, combine brown sugar, egg substitute, vanilla, creamer, and coffee and mix well. Add dry mixture to wet mixture and mix well.

Pour batter into pan. Bake for 40 minutes. Let cake cool for about 10 minutes before removing from pan.

Meanwhile, make glaze. Combine glaze ingredients and mix well. While cake is still very warm, put it back in pan. Poke holes in cake and pour glaze over it. Let cake soak in pan until completely cool. Remove from pan.

NUTRITIONAL INFORMATION PER SERVING			
Calories	255		
Protein	3.5 g	Dietary fiber	1 g
Carbohydrate	55 g	Cholesterol	0 mg
Fat	less than .5 g	Sodium	209 mg
Alcohol	2.3 g		
% Calories from fat	2%		

Vanilla Layer Cake

If you'd like, garnish this with fresh fruit.

14 SERVINGS

CAKE
Butter-flavored cooking spray
2¼ cups flour
¼ cup powdered sugar
1 teaspoon baking powder
1 teaspoon salt
2 cups sugar
½ cup fat-free egg substitute or 4 egg
  whites
1½ cups skim milk
2 teaspoons vanilla extract

ICING
1 7.2-ounce box fat-free fluffy white
  frosting mix
½ cup boiling water
1 teaspoon vanilla extract
2 tablespoons powdered sugar

Preheat oven to 325°F. Spray three 8½-inch round cake pans
with cooking spray and wipe with a paper towel to absorb the
excess.

In a medium-sized bowl, combine flour, powdered sugar,
baking powder, and salt and mix well. In a large bowl, combine
sugar, egg substitute, milk, and vanilla and mix well. Add the dry
mixture to the wet mixture and mix well. Spoon batter into the
three pans equally. Bake for 25 minutes. Let cakes cool for 5
minutes before removing from pans. Cool cakes completely.

To make icing, in a large bowl, combine frosting mix and boiling water. Beat until mix is melted. Beat on high until mixture is fluffy and stiff peaks form. Add vanilla and powdered sugar and beat well.

Assemble cake by covering two layers with icing. Stack these iced layers and top them with the plain layer. Spread the rest of the icing over the top and sides of cake. Refrigerate for several hours or overnight before serving.

NUTRITIONAL INFORMATION PER SERVING			
Calories	245		
Protein	4 g	Dietary fiber	less than .5 g
Carbohydrate	57 g	Cholesterol	0 mg
Fat	less than .5 g	Sodium	200 mg
% Calories from fat	1%		

POUND CAKE

10 SERVINGS

Butter-flavored cooking spray
3 cups flour
1½ cups powdered sugar
½ teaspoon baking powder
1½ teaspoons salt
½ cup plain nonfat yogurt
2 cups sugar
¼ cup fat-free egg substitute or *2 egg*
*   whites*
1 cup skim milk
2 teaspoons vanilla extract
1 teaspoon almond extract

Preheat oven to 300°F. Spray a loaf pan with cooking spray and wipe with a paper towel to spread cooking spray evenly and absorb the excess.

In a medium-sized bowl, combine flour, powdered sugar, baking powder, and salt and mix well. In a large bowl, combine remaining ingredients and mix well. Add dry mixture to wet mixture and mix well. Pour batter into pan. Bake for 1 hour and 55 minutes. Cool cake for 5 minutes before removing from pan. Remove cake and cool completely.

NUTRITIONAL INFORMATION PER SERVING			
Calories	381		
Protein	6 g	Dietary fiber	1 g
Carbohydrate	89 g	Cholesterol	less than 1 mg
Fat	less than .5 g	Sodium	351 mg
% Calories from fat	1%		

Cocoa Cola Cake

15 SERVINGS

CAKE

Butter-flavored cooking spray
2 cups flour
1 teaspoon baking soda
1 teaspoon salt
3 tablespoons unsweetened
   cocoa powder
2 cups sugar
½ cup fat-free egg substitute
   or 4 egg whites
½ cup nonfat buttermilk
1 teaspoon vanilla extract
1 cup cola soft drink

ICING

2 cups powdered sugar
⅛ teaspoon salt
2½ tablespoons unsweetened
   cocoa powder
¼ cup fat-free margarine
2 tablespoons cola soft drink
1 teaspoon vanilla extract

Preheat oven to 325°F. Spray a 13″ × 9″ pan with cooking spray and wipe with a paper towel. In a medium-sized bowl, combine flour, baking soda, salt, and cocoa and mix well. In a large bowl, combine sugar, egg substitute, buttermilk, vanilla, and cola and mix well. Add dry mixture to wet mixture and mix well. Pour batter into pan. Bake for 30 minutes. Cool cake completely.

Combine icing ingredients and mix well. Spread over cake.

NUTRITIONAL INFORMATION PER SERVING			
Calories	251		
Protein	3 g	Dietary fiber	1 g
Carbohydrate	59 g	Cholesterol	0 mg
Fat	less than .5 g	Sodium	290 mg
% Calories from fat	1%		

Boston Cream Cake

This is an easy dessert to make, and it has been a big hit with all who have tried it!

8 SERVINGS

CAKE
Butter-flavored cooking spray
1 cup flour
1 teaspoon baking powder
½ teaspoon salt
1 cup sugar
½ cup fat-free egg substitute or 4 egg
    whites
½ cup skim milk

CREAM FILLING
1 3.4-ounce box instant French vanilla
    pudding mix
1 cup skim milk

CHOCOLATE GLAZE
3 tablespoons unsweetened cocoa powder
1½ cups powdered sugar
⅛ teaspoon salt
3–4 tablespoons skim milk
1 teaspoon vanilla extract

Preheat oven to 325°F. Spray an 8½-inch round cake pan with cooking spray and wipe with a paper towel to absorb the excess. In a medium-sized bowl, combine flour, baking powder, and salt and mix well. In a large bowl, combine sugar, egg substitute, and milk. Mix well. Add dry mixture to wet mixture and mix well. Pour batter into pan. Bake for 30 minutes. Let cake cool for 5 minutes before removing from pan. Remove cake from pan and cool completely.

Make cream filling. In a medium-sized bowl, combine cream filling ingredients and mix well. Slice cooled cake in half horizontally, and spread the cream filling evenly over the bottom half of the cake. Place top half of the cake over the filling.

Make chocolate glaze. In a medium-sized bowl, combine cocoa, powdered sugar, and salt. Add milk and vanilla and mix well. Pour chocolate glaze over the cake and spread to cover the top and sides.

NUTRITIONAL INFORMATION PER SERVING			
Calories	320		
Protein	5 g	Dietary fiber	1.0 g
Carbohydrate	75 g	Cholesterol	less than 1 mg
Fat	less than .5 g	Sodium	276 mg
% Calories from fat	1%		

ORANGE MARMALADE CAKE

This is a very moist, delicious cake that combines the sweet tang of oranges with the mellow richness of vanilla.

12 SERVINGS

CAKE
Butter-flavored cooking spray
2 cups flour
1 teaspoon baking powder
1 teaspoon salt
1 11-ounce can mandarin orange
   segments, undrained
2 cups light brown sugar
1 teaspoon vanilla extract
½ cup fat-free egg substitute or 4 egg
   whites
¼ cup orange marmalade

TOPPING
1 3.4-ounce box instant vanilla pudding
   mix
1 cup skim milk
¾ cup orange marmalade

Preheat oven to 325°F. Spray a 13″ × 9″ pan with cooking spray and wipe with a paper towel to absorb the excess.

In a medium-sized bowl, combine flour, baking powder, and salt and mix well. Separate the orange segments from the liquid in the can. Reserve the orange segments. In a large bowl, combine brown sugar, vanilla, egg substitute, liquid from can of orange segments, and orange marmalade and mix well. Add dry mixture to wet mixture and mix well. Stir in reserved orange segments.

Pour batter into pan. Bake for 40 minutes.

Meanwhile, make topping. Combine pudding mix and milk and mix well. Add orange marmalade and mix well. Pour topping over warm cake and cool completely.

NUTRITIONAL INFORMATION PER SERVING			
Calories	346		
Protein	4 g	Dietary fiber	2.2 g
Carbohydrate	84 g	Cholesterol	less than .5 mg
Fat	less than .5 g	Sodium	274 mg
% Calories from fat	1%		

CARROT CAKE

For me, birthday celebrations have always been centered around food and family. When my sisters and I were kids, Mom would make our favorite meal, and Granny, a dear woman who abundantly expressed her affection with food and hugs, would appear at the door with our favorite dessert. Sweet, rich carrot cake was always my choice. This fat-free version is loaded with carrots, raisins, and pineapple and is now my birthday cake of choice each year! I like using whole-wheat flour in this recipe, which requires doubling the baking powder and baking soda, and adding a few walnuts to the batter. See the Index for chart that tells what this adds to the fat and calorie content per serving.

14 SERVINGS

ICING

1 cup nonfat sour cream
⅓ cup pineapple preserves
⅓ cup light brown sugar

¼ teaspoon coconut extract
⅔ cup powdered sugar

CAKE

Butter-flavored cooking spray
2¾ cups flour
½ teaspoon baking powder
½ teaspoon baking soda
½ teaspoon salt
1 teaspoon cinnamon
½ teaspoon allspice
½ teaspoon nutmeg
1 teaspoon ginger
1 cup light brown sugar
1 cup molasses

¼ cup fat-free egg substitute
    or 2 egg whites
¾ cup nonfat buttermilk
2 teaspoons vanilla extract
½ teaspoon coconut extract
1 8-ounce can crushed
    pineapple in syrup, drained
1 cup golden raisins
1–1½ pounds carrots, shredded
    coarse

To make icing, combine icing ingredients in a medium-sized bowl and mix well. Refrigerate uncovered.

Meanwhile, make cake. Preheat oven to 325°F. Spray three 8½-inch round cake pans with cooking spray and wipe with a paper towel to absorb the excess. In a medium-sized bowl combine flour, baking powder, baking soda, salt, and spices and mix well. In a large bowl, combine brown sugar, molasses, egg substitute, buttermilk, vanilla, coconut extract, and drained pineapple and mix well. Add raisins and carrots and stir well. Add the dry mixture to the wet mixture and mix well.

Spoon batter into the three pans equally. Bake for 40 minutes. Let cakes cool for 5-10 minutes before removing them from pans. Remove from pans and cool completely.

Assemble cake by covering two layers of cake with icing. Stack these iced layers and top them with the plain layer. Spread the rest of the icing over the top and sides of cake. Refrigerate for several hours or overnight before serving.

NUTRITIONAL INFORMATION PER SERVING			
Calories	356		
Protein	4.5 g	Dietary fiber	2 g
Carbohydrate	84 g	Cholesterol	0 mg
Fat	less than .5 g	Sodium	196 mg
% Calories from fat	1%		

Peach of a Cake

Made with fresh, ripe peaches, this moist, delicious cake is a summertime favorite.

12 SERVINGS

CAKE
Butter-flavored cooking spray
6–7 ripe peaches
5 tablespoons sugar
2 teaspoons cinnamon
3 cups flour
1 teaspoon salt
2 teaspoons baking powder
2 cups sugar
½ cup fat-free egg substitute or 4 egg whites
½ cup skim milk
½ cup light corn syrup
1 tablespoon frozen orange juice or lemonade concentrate, thawed
3 teaspoons vanilla extract

GLAZE
1 cup powdered sugar
Pinch of salt
Reserved peach liquid

Preheat oven to 300°F. Spray a Bundt pan thoroughly with cooking spray and wipe with a paper towel to spread cooking spray evenly and absorb the excess.

Cut unpeeled peaches into bite-sized chunks, toss with 5 tablespoons sugar and the cinnamon in a medium-sized bowl, and set aside. In a medium-sized bowl, combine flour, salt, and baking powder and mix well. In a large bowl, combine 2 cups sugar, egg substitute, milk, corn syrup, juice concentrate, vanilla, and 3 tablespoons of liquid from the peach mixture and mix well. Add dry mixture to wet mixture and mix well. Drain peaches, reserving the remaining liquid for use in glaze and stir peach chunks into the batter.

Spoon batter into pan. Bake for 1 hour and 30 minutes. Cool cake for 10 minutes before removing from pan. Remove cake from pan and cool completely.

Combine powdered sugar, salt, and reserved peach liquid. If necessary, add milk until you reach desired consistency. Drizzle glaze over cooled cake and serve.

NUTRITIONAL INFORMATION PER SERVING			
Calories	378		
Protein	4.5 g	Dietary fiber	1.5 g
Carbohydrate	90 g	Cholesterol	0 mg
Fat	less than .5 g	Sodium	219 mg
% Calories from fat	1%		

ORANGE CRANBERRY CAKE

This cake was a big hit with my taste-testing panel. It's simple to make and perfect for the holidays.

15 SERVINGS

CAKE

Butter-flavored cooking spray
2 cups flour
2 teaspoons baking powder
1 teaspoon salt
1 teaspoon cinnamon
½ cup quick oats
1 cup sugar
1 cup skim milk
¼ cup fat-free margarine

TOPPING

1 16-ounce can whole berry
   cranberry sauce
1 12-ounce jar orange
   marmalade

Preheat oven to 325°F. Spray a 13″ × 9″ pan with cooking spray and wipe with a paper towel. In a medium-sized bowl, combine flour, baking powder, salt, cinnamon, and oats and mix well. In a large bowl, combine sugar, milk, and margarine and mix well. Add dry mixture to wet mixture and mix well. Pour batter into pan. Bake for 30 minutes.

Meanwhile, make topping. Thoroughly stir together topping ingredients. Spread topping over warm cake.

NUTRITIONAL INFORMATION PER SERVING			
Calories	234		
Protein	3 g	Dietary fiber	2 g
Carbohydrate	57 g	Cholesterol	0 mg
Fat	less than .5 g	Sodium	177 mg
% Calories from fat	2%		

Butterscotch Oat Bars (recipe on page 29) ▶

BLACKBERRY CAKE

12 SERVINGS

CAKE
Butter-flavored cooking spray
2½ cups flour
1 cup powdered sugar
1 teaspoon baking powder
1 teaspoon salt
1 cup sugar
¾ cup nonfat buttermilk
*¼ cup fat-free egg substitute or 2 egg
   whites*
3 tablespoons blackberry brandy
¼ cup seedless blackberry jam

GLAZE
½ cup powdered sugar
Pinch of salt
1 tablespoon skim milk
1 tablespoon seedless blackberry jam

Preheat oven to 300°F. Spray a Bundt pan with cooking spray and wipe with a paper towel to absorb the excess. In a medium-sized bowl, combine flour, powdered sugar, baking powder, and salt and mix well. In a large bowl, combine sugar, buttermilk, egg substitute, and brandy and mix well. Add dry mixture to wet mixture and mix well.

   Spoon about one-half of batter into pan. Spoon jam in a ring in the middle of batter in pan. Spoon remaining batter into pan to cover jam. Bake for 50 minutes. Let cake cool for about 5 minutes before removing from pan.

Meanwhile, make icing. Combine icing ingredients and mix well. Drizzle icing over warm cake.

NUTRITIONAL INFORMATION PER SERVING			
Calories	260		
Protein	3.5 g	Dietary fiber	less than 1 g
Carbohydrate	59 g	Cholesterol	0 mg
Fat	less than .5 g	Sodium	214 mg
Alcohol	1 g		
% Calories from fat	1%		

Easy Apple Cinnamon Cake

This is a rich, moist dessert that's simple to make—no peeling or chopping!

12 SERVINGS

CAKE
Butter-flavored cooking spray
2 cups flour
1 teaspoon baking powder
2 teaspoons cinnamon
1 teaspoon salt
2 cups sugar
½ cup light corn syrup
½ cup fat-free egg substitute or 4 egg
  whites
1 tablespoon vanilla extract
1 21-ounce can apple pie filling

TOPPING
1 cup unsweetened apple sauce
1 cup powdered sugar
Pinch of salt
½ teaspoon vanilla extract

Preheat oven to 325°F. Spray a 13″ × 9″ pan with cooking spray and wipe with a paper towel to spread cooking spray evenly and absorb the excess.

In a medium-sized bowl, combine flour, baking powder, cinnamon, and salt and mix well. In a large bowl, combine sugar, corn syrup, egg substitute, and vanilla and mix well. Add dry mixture to wet mixture and mix well. This will result in a very stiff batter. Add pie filling and stir until well mixed. Pour batter into pan and spread evenly. Bake for 50 minutes.

After removing cake from oven, make topping. Combine topping ingredients and mix well. Pour topping over warm cake and spread evenly.

NUTRITIONAL INFORMATION PER SERVING			
Calories	354		
Protein	3 g	Dietary fiber	1 g
Carbohydrate	86 g	Cholesterol	0 mg
Fat	less than .5 g	Sodium	234 mg
% Calories from fat	1%		

LEMON POPPY SEED CAKE

This cake has a delicate lemon flavor and the crunch of poppy seeds, and the icing is sweet and tangy. If you'd like, you can add more poppy seeds. Add one-fourth cup poppy seeds for a cake with 1.3 grams of fat per serving.

14 SERVINGS

CAKE

Butter-flavored cooking spray
8 ounces plain nonfat yogurt
   (slightly less than 1 cup)
½ cup light corn syrup
3 cups sugar
1 teaspoon vanilla extract
1 cup fat-free egg substitute or
   8 egg whites
2 tablespoons fresh lemon
   juice
Rind from ½ lemon, grated
   fine
3 cups flour
⅓ cup powdered sugar
½ teaspoon baking powder
1 teaspoon salt
2 teaspoons poppy seeds

ICING

1 tablespoon fat-free
   margarine
2 tablespoons fresh lemon
   juice
Rind from ½ lemon, grated
   fine
½ teaspoon vanilla extract
⅛ teaspoon salt
2 cups powdered sugar
1 tablespoon skim milk

Preheat oven to 300°F. Spray a Bundt pan with cooking spray and wipe with a paper towel to absorb the excess.

In a large bowl, combine yogurt, corn syrup, sugar, vanilla, egg substitute, lemon juice, and lemon rind and mix well. In a medium-sized bowl, combine flour, powdered sugar, baking powder, and salt and mix well. Add dry mixture to wet mixture and mix well. Stir in poppy seeds. Pour batter into pan. Bake for 1 hour and 20 minutes.

Let cake cool for about 10 minutes before removing from pan. Remove cake from pan and cool in the refrigerator for about 15 minutes before icing.

Combine icing ingredients and mix well. Pour or spread icing over cake until it's completely covered. Cool cake in the refrigerator completely, preferably overnight, before serving.

NUTRITIONAL INFORMATION PER SERVING			
Calories	386		
Protein	5 g	Dietary fiber	less than 1 g
Carbohydrate	92 g	Cholesterol	0 mg
Fat	less than .5 g	Sodium	242 mg
% Calories from fat	1%		

Peach Rum Cake

12 SERVINGS

CAKE
Butter-flavored cooking spray
3 cups flour
1 teaspoon baking soda
1 teaspoon salt
1 teaspoon cinnamon
1 teaspoon nutmeg
2 cups sugar
¼ cup rum
¾ cup fat-free egg substitute or 6 egg
  whites
1 cup nonfat buttermilk
1 teaspoon vanilla extract
1 cup peach preserves

GLAZE
1½ cups powdered sugar
¼ teaspoon salt
5 tablespoons peach nectar
½ teaspoon rum extract

Preheat oven to 325°F. Spray a 13″ × 9″ pan with cooking spray and wipe with a paper towel to spread the cooking spray evenly and absorb the excess.

In a medium-sized bowl, combine flour, baking soda, salt, cinnamon, and nutmeg and mix well. In a large bowl, combine sugar, rum, egg substitute, buttermilk, and vanilla and mix well. Add dry mixture to wet mixture and mix well. Thoroughly stir in preserves. Pour batter into pan. Bake for 35 minutes.

After removing cake from oven, make glaze. Combine glaze ingredients and mix well. Poke holes in cake with a skewer and drizzle glaze over warm cake.

NUTRITIONAL INFORMATION PER SERVING			
Calories	394		
Protein	5 g	Dietary fiber	1 g
Carbohydrate	91 g	Cholesterol	0 mg
Fat	less than .5 g	Sodium	374 mg
Alcohol	1.5 g		
% Calories from fat	1%		

STRAWBERRY COCONUT CAKE

12 SERVINGS

CAKE

Butter-flavored cooking spray

3 cups flour

½ teaspoon baking powder

1 teaspoon salt

1 teaspoon cinnamon

2 cups sugar

1 cup fat-free egg substitute or *8 egg whites*

1 16-ounce package unsweetened frozen strawberries, thawed

¼ cup skim milk

2 teaspoons vanilla extract

1 teaspoon coconut extract

1 tablespoon flaked coconut, toasted (see Index)

GLAZE

1 cup powdered sugar

½ teaspoon vanilla extract

¼ teaspoon coconut extract

Pinch of salt

2½ tablespoons plain nonfat yogurt

Preheat oven to 325°F. Spray a Bundt pan thoroughly with cooking spray and wipe with a paper towel to spread cooking spray evenly and absorb the excess.

In a medium-sized bowl, combine flour, baking powder, salt, and cinnamon and mix well. In a large bowl, combine sugar, egg substitute, strawberries, milk, vanilla, coconut extract, and coconut and mix well, mashing the strawberries. Add dry mixture to wet mixture and mix well. Pour batter into pan. Bake for 55 minutes. Cool cake for 10 minutes before removing it from pan.

After removing cake from pan, make glaze. Combine glaze ingredients and drizzle glaze over warm cake.

NUTRITIONAL INFORMATION PER SERVING			
Calories	312		
Protein	5.5 g	Dietary fiber	2 g
Carbohydrate	72 g	Cholesterol	0 mg
Fat	less than .5 g	Sodium	222 mg
% Calories from fat	1%		

Fresh Blueberry Cake

A special thanks goes to my husband's grandmother, Olive Beach, who was kind enough to give me her delicious blueberry cake recipe, which I modified to make fat-free.

12 SERVINGS

Butter-flavored cooking spray	1 tablespoon vanilla extract
3 cups flour	¼ cup fat-free egg substitute
2 teaspoons baking powder	or 2 egg whites
½ teaspoon salt	1 cup blueberries
2 cups sugar	1 cup flour to coat berries
1½ cups skim milk	

Preheat oven to 300°F. Spray a Bundt pan with cooking spray and wipe with a paper towel to absorb the excess. In a medium-sized bowl, combine 3 cups flour, baking powder, and salt and mix well. In a large bowl, combine sugar, milk, vanilla, and egg substitute and mix well. Add dry mixture to wet mixture and mix well.

Rinse blueberries and gently pat until mostly dry. Put blueberries in a medium-sized bowl with 1 cup flour and gently toss to cover the berries. Strain excess flour from berries. Add berries to batter and stir gently. Pour batter into pan. Bake for 55 minutes. Let cake cool for 5 minutes before removing from pan.

NUTRITIONAL INFORMATION PER SERVING			
Calories	271		
Protein	5 g	Dietary fiber	1 g
Carbohydrate	62 g	Cholesterol	.5 mg
Fat	less than .5 g	Sodium	116 mg
% Calories from fat	1%		

Chocolate Fudge Layer Cake (recipe on pages 42–43) ▶

Banana Split Cake

This cake contains the unique blend of flavors that makes a banana split such a special treat. Try it with a scoop of low-fat vanilla ice cream and a sprinkling of chopped nuts. See Index for chart that tells what the addition of nuts adds to the fat and calorie content per serving.

12 SERVINGS

Butter-flavored cooking spray
Flour to coat pan
3 cups flour
1 teaspoon baking soda
1 teaspoon salt
2 cups sugar
1 cup strawberry syrup
¾ cup fat-free egg substitute or 6 egg
   whites
2 teaspoons vanilla extract
2 bananas, diced
1 10-ounce jar maraschino cherries,
   drained, chopped
1 8-ounce can pineapple chunks, drained
1 11½-ounce jar fat-free hot fudge topping

Preheat oven to 325°F. Spray a 13″ × 9″ pan with cooking spray and wipe with a paper towel to spread cooking spray evenly and absorb the excess. Dust pan with flour and shake out the excess.

In a medium-sized bowl, combine flour, baking soda, and salt and mix well. In a large bowl, combine sugar, strawberry syrup, egg substitute, and vanilla and mix well. Add dry mixture to wet mixture and mix well. Stir in bananas, cherries, and pineapple.

Pour batter into pan and spread evenly. Bake for 50 minutes.

Cool cake for 10–15 minutes. Spread hot fudge sauce evenly over cake.

NUTRITIONAL INFORMATION PER SERVING			
Calories	413		
Protein	6 g	Dietary fiber	1.5 g
Carbohydrate	99 g	Cholesterol	0 mg
Fat	less than .5 g	Sodium	335 mg
% Calories from fat	1%		

PINEAPPLE UPSIDE-DOWN CAKE

12 SERVINGS

1 cup light brown sugar
¼ cup pure maple syrup
¼ cup skim milk
10 slices canned pineapple in
  heavy syrup
12 maraschino cherries
1½ cups flour
½ teaspoon baking powder

½ teaspoon salt
Reserved pineapple syrup
1 cup sugar
¼ cup fat-free egg substitute
  or 2 egg whites
2 teaspoons vanilla extract
¼ cup skim milk

Preheat oven to 325°F. In a small bowl, combine brown sugar, maple syrup, and ¼ cup milk and mix well. Spread mixture over the bottom of a 13″ × 9″ pan. Drain pineapple slices and reserve ¾ cup syrup. Arrange eight whole pineapple slices, two slices that have been cut in half, and cherries over mixture in pan.

In a medium-sized bowl, combine flour, baking powder, and salt and mix well. In a large bowl, combine reserved pineapple syrup, sugar, egg substitute, vanilla, and ¼ cup milk and mix well. Add dry mixture to wet mixture and mix well. Pour batter evenly over fruit in pan. Bake for 35 minutes. Cool cake in pan for 2 minutes. Invert cake onto a large serving plate.

NUTRITIONAL INFORMATION PER SERVING			
Calories	258		
Protein	2.5 g	Dietary fiber	less than 1 g
Carbohydrate	62 g	Cholesterol	0 mg
Fat	less than .5 g	Sodium	110 mg
% Calories from fat	1%		

5

Pies

FUDGE SWIRL PIE

The rich swirl of fudge in this pie makes it look as good as it tastes!

8 SERVINGS

CRUST
Butter-flavored cooking spray
20 fat-free wheat crackers
½ cup powdered sugar
⅓ cup plain nonfat yogurt

FILLING
½ cup flour
*½ cup fat-free egg substitute or 4 egg
    whites*
1 cup sugar
¼ teaspoon salt
2 teaspoons vanilla extract

FUDGE SWIRL
¾ cup powdered sugar
¼ cup unsweetened cocoa powder
Pinch of salt
2 tablespoons skim milk
½ teaspoon vanilla extract
2 teaspoons fat-free margarine

Preheat oven to 325°F. Spray a 9-inch deep-dish pie pan with cooking spray and wipe with a paper towel to spread cooking spray evenly and absorb the excess. Put crackers and powdered sugar in food processor. Process to make fine crumbs. In a medium-sized bowl, combine crumb mixture with yogurt and mix until crumbs are evenly moistened. Press crumbs evenly into the bottom and partway up the side of pie pan.

In a medium-sized bowl, combine the filling ingredients and mix well. Pour filling over piecrust.

In a medium-sized bowl, combine the fudge swirl ingredients and mix well. Spoon fudge swirl in thick horizontal and vertical stripes over pie filling and swirl with a fork or spoon. Bake for 30 minutes. Cool completely.

NUTRITIONAL INFORMATION PER SERVING			
Calories	255		
Protein	4.5 g	Dietary fiber	1.5 g
Carbohydrate	58 g	Cholesterol	0 mg
Fat	less than .5 g	Sodium	202 mg
% Calories from fat	1%		

Banana Custard Pie

This is not a particularly attractive pie, but you won't mind once you taste the delightful custard filling, which is complemented by an oatmeal cookie crust.

8 SERVINGS

CRUST
Butter-flavored cooking spray
6–7 ounces fat-free soft oatmeal cookies
¼ cup plain nonfat yogurt

FILLING
2 very ripe bananas
¾ cup sugar
½ cup nonfat dry milk powder
1 tablespoon cornstarch
1 teaspoon vanilla extract
½ teaspoon coconut extract
¼ teaspoon salt
½ cup fat-free egg substitute or 4 egg
   whites
1 cup skim milk

Preheat oven to 325°F. Spray a 9-inch deep-dish pie pan with cooking spray and wipe with a paper towel to spread cooking spray evenly and absorb the excess. Use a food processor to make crumbs of cookies. Mix crumbs with yogurt and press mixture into the bottom of pan (not up the side).

Mash bananas with a fork in a large bowl. Add remaining filling ingredients except skim milk and mix well. Add skim milk and mix until dry milk is completely dissolved. Pour filling into pie pan. Bake for 45 minutes. Chill pie completely.

NUTRITIONAL INFORMATION PER SERVING			
Calories	223		
Protein	5 g	Dietary fiber	1 g
Carbohydrate	50 g	Cholesterol	1.4 mg
Fat	less than .5 g	Sodium	272 mg
% Calories from fat	1%		

PINEAPPLE-COCONUT CREAM PIE

8 SERVINGS

CRUST
Butter-flavored cooking spray
20 fat-free wheat crackers
½ cup powdered sugar
⅓ cup plain nonfat yogurt

FILLING
16 ounces plain nonfat yogurt, drained
  (see Index)
½ cup sugar
½ teaspoon salt
½ teaspoon vanilla extract
½ teaspoon coconut extract
¼ cup skim milk
½ cup fat-free egg substitute or 4 egg
  whites
12 ounces pineapple preserves (about 1
  cup)
2 tablespoons flaked coconut

Preheat oven to 325°F. Spray a 9-inch deep-dish pie pan with cooking spray and wipe with a paper towel to spread cooking spray evenly and absorb the excess. Put crackers and powdered sugar in a food processor. Process to make fine crumbs. In a medium-sized bowl, combine crumb mixture with yogurt and mix until evenly moistened. Press crumbs evenly into the bottom and partway up the side of pie pan.

In a large bowl, combine drained yogurt, sugar, and salt and mix well. Add vanilla, coconut extract, milk, and egg substitute

and mix well. Add preserves and coconut and mix well. Pour
filling over piecrust. Bake for 50 minutes. Cool pie completely.

NUTRITIONAL INFORMATION PER SERVING			
Calories	264		
Protein	6 g	Dietary fiber	1 g
Carbohydrate	60 g	Cholesterol	1.5 mg
Fat	less than .5 g	Sodium	267 mg
% Calories from fat	1%		

BUTTERMILK PIE

8 SERVINGS

CRUST
Butter-flavored cooking spray
20 fat-free wheat crackers
½ cup powdered sugar
⅓ cup plain nonfat yogurt

FILLING
1 cup nonfat buttermilk
1 cup sugar
¼ teaspoon salt
1 teaspoon vanilla extract
1 tablespoon cornstarch
¼ cup fat-free egg substitute
  or 2 egg whites
Sprinkle of nutmeg

Preheat oven to 325°F. Spray a 9-inch deep-dish pie pan with cooking spray and wipe with a paper towel. Put crackers and powdered sugar in a food processor. Process to make fine crumbs. In a medium-sized bowl, combine crumb mixture with yogurt and mix until evenly moistened. Press crumbs evenly into the bottom and partway up the side of pie pan.

In a large bowl, combine buttermilk, sugar, salt, vanilla, and cornstarch and mix well. Add egg substitute and mix well. Pour filling over piecrust. Sprinkle nutmeg over the top of pie filling. Bake for 40 minutes. Cool pie completely.

NUTRITIONAL INFORMATION PER SERVING			
Calories	179		
Protein	3 g	Dietary fiber	.5 g
Carbohydrate	42 g	Cholesterol	less than 1 mg
Fat	less than .5 g	Sodium	197 mg
% Calories from fat	1%		

CHOCOLATE CREAM PIE

This recipe yields a delicious pie with a smooth, creamy filling.

8 SERVINGS

CRUST

Butter-flavored cooking spray
20 fat-free wheat crackers
½ cup powdered sugar
2 tablespoons unsweetened
  cocoa powder
5 tablespoons skim milk

FILLING

1 cup sugar
¼ cup unsweetened cocoa
  powder
¼ teaspoon salt
1 teaspoon vanilla extract
1 tablespoon cornstarch
¼ cup fat-free egg substitute
  or 2 egg whites
1 cup skim milk

Preheat oven to 325°F. Spray a 9-inch deep-dish pie pan with cooking spray and wipe with a paper towel. Put crackers, powdered sugar, and cocoa in a food processor. Process to make fine crumbs. In a medium-sized bowl, combine crumb mixture with milk and mix until evenly moistened. Press crumbs evenly into the bottom and partway up the side of pan.

In a large bowl, combine all filling ingredients except milk and mix well. Add milk and mix well. Pour filling over piecrust. Bake for 40 minutes. Cool pie completely.

NUTRITIONAL INFORMATION PER SERVING			
Calories	193		
Protein	4 g	Dietary fiber	1.5 g
Carbohydrate	43 g	Cholesterol	less than 1 mg
Fat	less than .5 g	Sodium	179 mg
% Calories from fat	2%		

STRAWBERRY SWIRL PIE

8 SERVINGS

CRUST
Butter-flavored cooking spray
20 fat-free wheat crackers
½ cup powdered sugar
⅓ cup plain nonfat yogurt

FILLING
½ cup flour
½ teaspoon baking powder
¼ teaspoon salt
⅓ cup sugar
¼ cup fat-free egg substitute or 2 egg
   whites
½ teaspoon vanilla extract
¼ cup skim milk
1 10-ounce package frozen strawberries in
   syrup, thawed and pureed

Preheat oven to 325°F. Spray a 9-inch deep-dish pie pan with
cooking spray and wipe with a paper towel to spread cooking
spray evenly and absorb the excess. Put crackers and powdered
sugar in a food processor. Process to make fine crumbs. In a
medium-sized bowl, combine crumb mixture with yogurt and
mix until evenly moistened. Press crumbs evenly into the bottom and partway up the side of pie pan.

   In a medium-sized bowl, combine all filling ingredients except pureed strawberries and mix well. Pour strawberries over

piecrust. Spoon filling over strawberries in the pan. Swirl filling with strawberries. Bake for 40 minutes. Cool pie completely.

NUTRITIONAL INFORMATION PER SERVING			
Calories	158		
Protein	3.5 g	Dietary fiber	1.5 g
Carbohydrate	36 g	Cholesterol	0 mg
Fat	less than .5 g	Sodium	170 mg
% Calories from fat	1%		

BLUEBERRIES-AND-CREAM PIE

8 SERVINGS

CRUST
1 cup wheat and barley nugget cereal
⅓ cup powdered sugar
4 tablespoons plain nonfat yogurt

FILLING
1 cup nonfat sour cream
2 tablespoons flour
¾ cup sugar
1 teaspoon vanilla extract
¼ teaspoon salt
¼ cup fat-free egg substitute or 2 egg
    whites
2 cups fresh blueberries, rinsed and dried

CRUMB TOPPING
4 tablespoons flour
4 tablespoons light brown sugar
⅛ teaspoon salt
½–1 tablespoon plain nonfat yogurt

Preheat oven to 400°F. Combine crust ingredients and mix well. Spread crust mixture evenly over bottom of a 9-inch deep-dish pie pan.

Combine all filling ingredients except the blueberries and mix well. Fold in blueberries. Pour filling into pie pan. Bake for 25 minutes.

Meanwhile, combine crumb topping ingredients and mix until crumbly. After pie has baked for 25 minutes, sprinkle topping over hot pie. Bake pie an additional 10 minutes. Chill pie completely before serving.

NUTRITIONAL INFORMATION PER SERVING			
Calories	251		
Protein	5 g	Dietary fiber	3 g
Carbohydrate	57 g	Cholesterol	0 mg
Fat	less than .5 g	Sodium	250 mg
% Calories from fat	1%		

KEY LIME PIE

This recipe makes a rich and creamy pie. It's a great way to cap a spicy meal.

8 SERVINGS

CRUST
Butter-flavored cooking spray
15 fat-free wheat crackers
2 reduced-fat vanilla sandwich cookies
⅔ cup powdered sugar
2 tablespoons fat-free margarine

FILLING
16 ounces plain nonfat yogurt, drained
  (see Index)
1 cup nonfat sour cream
¼ teaspoon salt
1 teaspoon vanilla extract
3 tablespoons light corn syrup
1 cup nonfat dry milk powder
1 tablespoon cornstarch
⅓ cup skim milk
⅔ cup sugar
½ cup Key lime juice

Put crackers, cookies, and powdered sugar in a food processor. Process to make fine crumbs. Mix crumb mixture with margarine until evenly moistened. Press crumb mixture into the bottom of a 9-inch deep-dish pie pan (not up the side).

Combine drained yogurt, sour cream, salt, vanilla, corn syrup, and dry milk in a large bowl and mix well. In a medium-sized saucepan, mix cornstarch with skim milk. Add sugar and lime juice to milk mixture and bring to a boil over medium heat, stirring constantly. Boil, stirring constantly, for 1 minute. Add hot mixture to mixture in large bowl and mix well. Pour filling over crust and refrigerate until completely chilled.

NUTRITIONAL INFORMATION PER SERVING			
Calories	260		
Protein	8 g	Dietary fiber	.5 g
Carbohydrate	55 g	Cholesterol	2.8 mg
Fat	less than .5 g	Sodium	284 mg
% Calories from fat	1%		

Cherry-Vanilla Cream Pie

This pie reminds me of one of my dad's favorites, except, of course, that this pie is fat-free while the other recipe is loaded with saturated fat. This pie was very popular with my taste-testing panel. If you'd like, add some chopped, toasted almonds to the crust. See the index for chart that tells what this would add to the fat and calorie content per serving.

8 SERVINGS

CRUST
Butter-flavored cooking spray
15 fat-free wheat crackers
1½ reduced-fat vanilla sandwich cookies
⅔ cup powdered sugar
2 tablespoons fat-free margarine

FILLING
*1 3.4-ounce box instant vanilla pudding
  mix*
½ cup skim milk
1 cup nonfat sour cream
⅛ teaspoon almond extract
1 21-ounce can cherry pie filling

Spray a 9-inch deep-dish pie pan with cooking spray and wipe with a paper towel to spread cooking spray evenly and absorb the excess. Put crackers, cookies, and powdered sugar in a food processor. Process to make fine crumbs. In a medium-sized bowl, combine crumb mixture with margarine and mix until evenly moistened. Press crumbs evenly into the bottom of pie pan (not up the side).

In a large bowl, combine all filling ingredients and mix well.

Pour evenly over pie crust. Spoon cherry pie filling evenly over
pudding mixture in pan. Chill pie for several hours before
serving.

NUTRITIONAL INFORMATION PER SERVING			
Calories	198		
Protein	2.5 g	Dietary fiber	1 g
Carbohydrate	45 g	Cholesterol	less than .5 g
Fat	less than .5 g	Sodium	187 mg
% Calories from fat	2%		

Mocha Pie

8 SERVINGS

CRUST
Butter-flavored cooking spray
15 fat-free wheat crackers
2 reduced-fat chocolate sandwich cookies
⅔ cup powdered sugar
2 tablespoons fat-free margarine

FILLING
1 3.4-ounce box instant vanilla pudding
* mix*
1 tablespoon unsweetened cocoa powder
1 teaspoon instant coffee granules
1 12-ounce can evaporated skimmed milk

Spray a 9-inch deep-dish pie pan with cooking spray and wipe with a paper towel to spread cooking spray evenly and absorb the excess. Put crackers, cookies, and powdered sugar in a food processor. Process to make fine crumbs. In a medium-sized bowl, combine crumb mixture with margarine and mix until evenly moistened. Press crumbs evenly into the bottom of pie pan (not up the side).

In a large bowl, combine all filling ingredients and mix well. Pour filling over piecrust. Chill for several hours before serving.

NUTRITIONAL INFORMATION PER SERVING			
Calories	158		
Protein	4.5 g	Dietary fiber	.5g
Carbohydrate	34 g	Cholesterol	1.5 g
Fat	less than .5 g	Sodium	238 mg
% Calories from fat	3%		

MAPLE ICE CREAM–WAFFLE PIE

Make sure you use pure maple syrup, not maple-flavored syrup, in this recipe. With only 174 calories per serving, this pie is a good excuse to add dessert to your breakfast routine!

8 SERVINGS

CRUST
Butter-flavored cooking spray
4 fat-free frozen waffles,
   toasted
¼ cup pure maple syrup
1 tablespoon fat-free
   margarine

FILLING
1 quart (4 cups) fat-free
   vanilla ice cream
¼ cup maple syrup

Spray a 9-inch deep-dish pie pan with cooking spray and wipe with a paper towel to spread cooking spray evenly and absorb the excess. Use a food processor to make crumbs of toasted waffles. In a medium-sized bowl, combine maple syrup and margarine and mix well. Add waffle crumbs and stir until evenly moistened. Spread crumbs evenly over the bottom of pie pan.

Spoon ice cream into a large bowl and stir until smooth enough to spread. Spread ice cream over crust. Drizzle maple syrup over ice cream. Freeze pie until ice cream hardens again.

NUTRITIONAL INFORMATION PER SERVING			
Calories	174		
Protein	4.5 g	Dietary fiber	0 g
Carbohydrate	39 g	Cholesterol	less than 1 g
Fat	less than .5 g	Sodium	126 mg
% Calories from fat	1%		

GRASSHOPPER PIE

This cool, creamy pie, with a mild blend of mint and cocoa, is a delightful summer dessert.

8 SERVINGS

CRUST
Butter-flavored cooking spray
15 fat-free wheat crackers
2 reduced-fat chocolate sandwich cookies
⅔ cup powdered sugar
1 tablespoon unsweetened cocoa powder
2 tablespoons fat-free margarine

FILLING
1 7.2-ounce box fat-free fluffy white
   frosting mix
⅓ cup boiling water
2 tablespoons crème de menthe
2 tablespoons crème de cacao
½ cup powdered sugar
16 ounces plain nonfat yogurt, drained
   (see Index)
½ teaspoon unsweetened cocoa powder

Spray a 9-inch deep-dish pie pan with cooking spray and wipe with a paper towel to spread cooking spray evenly and absorb the excess. Put crackers, cookies, powdered sugar, and cocoa in a food processor. Process to make fine crumbs. In a medium-sized bowl, combine crumb mixture with margarine and mix until evenly moistened. Press crumbs evenly into the bottom of pie pan (not up the side).

In a large bowl, combine frosting mix and boiling water and

mix on low speed until powder is dissolved. Beat on high speed
for about 5 minutes until mixture is stiff. Add crème de menthe,
crème de cacao, and powdered sugar and mix well. Add drained
yogurt and mix well. Pour filling evenly over piecrust. Dust with
cocoa. Chill for several hours, and then freeze for at least 5
hours.

NUTRITIONAL INFORMATION PER SERVING			
Calories	255		
Protein	4.5 g	Dietary fiber	.5 g
Carbohydrate	55 g	Cholesterol	1 mg
Fat	less than .5 g	Sodium	193 mg
Alcohol	2.5 g		
% Calories from fat	1%		

PUMPKIN PIE

The aroma of pumpkin pie baking is almost as satisfying as its taste. While most pumpkin pies have low-fat fillings, the crusts are quite high in fat. You won't want to wait until the holiday season to make this delicious, traditional fat-free pie.

8 SERVINGS

CRUST
Butter-flavored cooking spray
20 fat-free wheat crackers
½ cup powdered sugar
⅓ cup plain nonfat yogurt

FILLING
1 16-ounce can solid-pack pumpkin
1¾ cups skim milk
½ cup fat-free egg substitute or 4 egg
    whites
1 cup sugar
1 teaspoon cinnamon
½ teaspoon nutmeg
½ teaspoon ginger
1 teaspoon vanilla extract
½ teaspoon salt

Preheat oven to 325°F. Spray a 9-inch deep-dish pie pan with cooking spray and wipe with a paper towel to spread cooking spray evenly and absorb the excess. Use food processor to make crumbs of crackers. In a medium-sized bowl, mix cracker crumbs with powdered sugar. Add yogurt and mix until evenly moistened. Press crumb mixture evenly into the bottom and partway up the side of the pie pan.

In a large bowl, combine filling ingredients and mix well. Pour filling over crust. Bake for 55 minutes. Cool completely before serving.

NUTRITIONAL INFORMATION PER SERVING			
Calories	207		
Protein	5 g	Dietary fiber	2 g
Carbohydrate	47 g	Cholesterol	1 mg
Fat	less than .5 g	Sodium	272 mg
% Calories from fat	1%		

SWEET POTATO PIE

8 SERVINGS

CRUST
Butter-flavored cooking spray
20 fat-free wheat crackers
½ cup powdered sugar
⅓ cup plain nonfat yogurt

FILLING
1 16-ounce can sweet potatoes in syrup
½ cup nonfat buttermilk
½ cup fat-free egg substitute or 4 egg
* whites*
1 cup sugar
½ teaspoon cinnamon
½ teaspoon nutmeg
½ teaspoon salt
½ teaspoon baking soda
½ teaspoon baking powder

Preheat oven to 300°F. Spray a 9-inch deep-dish pie pan with cooking spray and wipe with a paper towel to spread cooking spray evenly and absorb the excess. Put crackers and powdered sugar in a food processor. Process to make fine crumbs. In a medium-sized bowl, combine crumb mixture with yogurt and mix until evenly moistened. Press crumbs evenly into the bottom and partway up the side of the pie pan.

Put sweet potatoes and liquid from the can in a large bowl. Use a fork to mash the sweet potato chunks. Add buttermilk and egg substitute and mix well. In a small bowl, mix together the sugar, cinnamon, nutmeg, salt, baking soda, and baking powder.

Add the dry mixture to the sweet potato mixture and mix well.
Pour pie filling over crust. Bake for 1 hour and 10 minutes. Cool
completely before serving.

NUTRITIONAL INFORMATION PER SERVING			
Calories	228		
Protein	4 g	Dietary fiber	1.3 g
Carbohydrate	54.5 g	Cholesterol	0 mg
Fat	less than .5 g	Sodium	362 mg
% Calories from fat	1%		

FRUIT CRUNCH PIE

*Use a mixture of dried fruit bits in this recipe for a variety of
flavors in each bite. For a tangy burst of flavor, use only dried
apricots.*

8 SERVINGS

FILLING
2 6-ounce packages dried fruit, chopped
1 6-ounce can frozen orange juice
   concentrate, thawed
⅔ cup boiling water
1 cup sugar
¼ teaspoon salt
1 teaspoon vanilla extract
½ teaspoon cinnamon
¾ cup fat-free egg substitute or 6 egg
   whites

CRUST
Butter-flavored cooking spray
10 fat-free wheat crackers
½ cup powdered sugar
¼ teaspoon cinnamon
2 tablespoons fat-free margarine

CRUNCH TOPPING
½ cup flour
½ cup light brown sugar
¼ teaspoon salt
¼ teaspoon cinnamon
1½ tablespoons plain nonfat yogurt

Combine dried fruit bits, orange juice concentrate, and boiling water. Cover and let sit overnight.

To make crust, preheat oven to 325°F. Spray a 9-inch deep-dish pie pan with cooking spray and wipe with a paper towel to spread cooking spray evenly and absorb the excess. Put crackers, powdered sugar, and cinnamon in a food processor. Process to make fine crumbs. In a medium-sized bowl, combine crumb mixture with margarine and mix until evenly moistened. Press crumbs evenly into the bottom of pie pan (not up the side).

To make filling, in a large bowl, combine sugar, salt, vanilla, cinnamon, and egg substitute and mix well. Add the fruit mixture and mix well. Pour filling over pie crust.

In a medium-sized bowl, combine topping ingredients and mix until crumbs are moistened. Sprinkle topping evenly over filling. Bake for 35 minutes. Cool completely.

NUTRITIONAL INFORMATION PER SERVING			
Calories	385		
Protein	5 g	Dietary fiber	3 g
Carbohydrate	94 g	Cholesterol	0 mg
Fat	less than .5 g	Sodium	252 mg
% Calories from fat	1%		

6

Breads, Muffins, Cupcakes, and Coffee Cakes

AUNT OUIDA'S CRANBERRY BREAD

My great-great-aunt Ouida was an eccentric, fun-loving woman who wore loud jewelry and made perfect cranberry bread. My skeptical family couldn't taste any difference between her cranberry bread and my healthier version, and my husband just craves this stuff! Although Aunt Ouida's recipe calls for regular flour, this fat-free recipe tastes more like hers when its made with whole-wheat flour.

10 SERVINGS

Butter-flavored cooking spray
2 cups flour
½ teaspoon salt
½ teaspoon baking powder
½ teaspoon baking soda
¼ cup fat-free egg substitute or 2 egg
   whites
1½ cups sugar
1 tablespoon vanilla extract
½ cup orange juice
2 tablespoons light corn syrup
1 12-ounce bag fresh or frozen cranberries
Rind from 1 orange, grated fine

Preheat oven to 325°F. Spray a loaf pan with cooking spray and wipe with a paper towel to absorb the excess.

In a medium-sized bowl, mix together flour, salt, baking powder, and baking soda. In a large bowl, combine egg substitute, sugar, vanilla, orange juice, and corn syrup and mix well. Add the dry mixture to the wet mixture and mix well. If you're using frozen cranberries, do not thaw them before rinsing.

Coarsely chop cranberries in a food processor or by hand. Add cranberries and orange rind to batter and mix well.

Pour batter into pan. If you're using fresh cranberries, bake for 45–50 minutes. If you're using frozen cranberries, bake for 60–70 minutes. Cool bread for about 5 minutes before removing from pan.

NUTRITIONAL INFORMATION PER SERVING			
Calories	249		
Protein	3 g	Dietary fiber	2 g
Carbohydrate	59 g	Cholesterol	0 mg
Fat	less than .5 g	Sodium	183 mg
% Calories from fat	1%		

DATE BREAD

10 SERVINGS

2 8-ounce packages chopped
   dates
1 cup water
Butter-flavored cooking spray
Flour to coat pan
2 cups flour
2 teaspoons baking powder

1 teaspoon salt
1½ cups sugar
¼ cup fat-free egg substitute
   or 2 egg whites
½ cup apple butter
1 teaspoon vanilla extract

Preheat oven to 300°F. In a medium-sized sauce pan, stir together dates and water. Cover and bring to a simmer over medium heat. Simmer for 3 minutes. Remove from heat.

Spray a loaf pan with cooking spray and wipe with paper towel to spread cooking spray evenly and absorb the excess. Dust pan with flour and shake out the excess.

In a medium-sized bowl, combine 2 cups flour, baking powder, and salt and mix well. In a large bowl, combine sugar, egg substitute, apple butter, and vanilla and mix well. Add dry mixture to wet mixture and mix well. Add date mixture and mix well. Pour batter into pan. Bake for 1 hour and 25 minutes. Cool in pan for 5 minutes, then remove bread from pan.

NUTRITIONAL INFORMATION PER SERVING			
Calories	347		
Protein	4 g	Dietary fiber	5 g
Carbohydrate	86 g	Cholesterol	0 mg
Fat	less than .5 g	Sodium	228 mg
% Calories from fat	1%		

Vanilla Layer Cake (recipe on pages 62–63) ▶

SUMMERTIME GINGERBREAD

*This gingerbread snack cake is extra moist and tasty due to the
fresh nectarines.*

12 SERVINGS

Butter-flavored cooking spray
1⅔ cups flour
½ teaspoon baking soda
1½ teaspoons ginger
¾ teaspoon cinnamon
¾ teaspoon salt
¼ cup fat-free egg substitute
   or 2 egg whites

½ cup sugar
1 cup molasses
⅓ cup plain nonfat yogurt
1 teaspoon vanilla extract
4–5 medium-sized ripe
   nectarines
2 tablespoons powdered sugar
   to dust cake

Preheat oven to 325°F. Spray a 13″ × 9″ pan with cooking spray
and wipe with a paper towel.

In a small bowl, mix together flour, baking soda, ginger,
cinnamon, and salt. In a large bowl, combine egg substitute,
sugar, molasses, yogurt, and vanilla and mix well. Add dry
mixture to wet mixture and mix well. Chop nectarines into
small pieces. Stir nectarine pieces into batter.

Pour batter into pan. Bake for 35 minutes. Cool cake completely. Dust with powdered sugar.

NUTRITIONAL INFORMATION PER SERVING			
Calories	195		
Protein	3 g	Dietary fiber	1 g
Carbohydrate	46 g	Cholesterol	0 mg
Fat	less than .5 g	Sodium	208 mg
% Calories from fat	2%		

PUMPKIN RAISIN BREAD

12 SERVINGS

Butter-flavored cooking spray

2 cups flour

1½ tablespoons quick oats

1 tablespoon baking powder

½ teaspoon baking soda

¾ teaspoon salt

1 teaspoon cinnamon

¼ teaspoon nutmeg

1 cup sugar

⅓ cup light brown sugar

1¼ cups skim milk

1 16-ounce can solid-pack pumpkin

¼ cup fat-free egg substitute or 2 egg whites

1 teaspoon vanilla extract

1 cup raisins

Preheat oven to 325°F. Spray a loaf pan with cooking spray and wipe with a paper towel to spread cooking spray evenly and absorb the excess.

In a medium-sized bowl, combine flour, oats, baking powder, baking soda, salt, cinnamon, and nutmeg and mix well. In a large bowl, combine sugar, brown sugar, milk, pumpkin, egg substitute, and vanilla and mix well. Add dry mixture to wet mixture and mix well. Stir in raisins. Pour batter into pan. Bake for 1 hour and 10 minutes. Cool bread in pan for 5 minutes, then remove from pan.

NUTRITIONAL INFORMATION PER SERVING			
Calories	229		
Protein	4 g	Dietary fiber	2 g
Carbohydrate	53 g	Cholesterol	0 mg
Fat	less than .5 g	Sodium	164 mg
% Calories from fat	2%		

Banana Bread

If you'd like, add some nuts to your banana bread. See the Index for chart that tells what this would add to the fat and calorie content per serving.

12 SERVINGS

Butter-flavored cooking spray
2 cups flour
¾ cup powdered sugar
½ teaspoon baking powder
¼ teaspoon baking soda
½ teaspoon salt
½ teaspoon nutmeg
½ teaspoon cinnamon

3 very ripe medium-sized
    bananas or 2 very large
    ripe bananas
1 tablespoon fresh lemon
    juice
1 cup light brown sugar
1 cup nonfat buttermilk
1 tablespoon vanilla extract

Preheat oven to 325°F. Spray a loaf pan with cooking spray and wipe with a paper towel.

In a medium-sized bowl, combine flour, powdered sugar, baking powder, baking soda, salt, nutmeg, and cinnamon and mix well. In a large bowl, mash bananas with lemon juice. Add brown sugar, buttermilk, and vanilla and mix well. Add dry mixture to wet mixture and mix well. Pour batter into pan. Bake for 1 hour and 15 minutes.

Cool bread in pan for 5 minutes, then remove from pan.

NUTRITIONAL INFORMATION PER SERVING			
Calories	213		
Protein	3 g	Dietary fiber	1 g
Carbohydrate	49 g	Cholesterol	0 mg
Fat	less than .5 g	Sodium	145 mg
% Calories from fat	2%		

Pound Cake (recipe on page 64) with Caramel Sauce (recipe on page 182) ▶

BLUEBERRY MUFFINS

These muffins are moist, delicious, and bursting with blueberries.

12 SERVINGS / 1 MUFFIN PER SERVING

2 cups fresh blueberries

Powdered sugar to coat
    blueberries

2 cups flour

½ cup powdered sugar

1 teaspoon baking powder

½ teaspoon salt

½ teaspoon nutmeg

½ teaspoon cinnamon

1 cup dark brown sugar

1 teaspoon vanilla extract

1 cup skim milk

Preheat oven to 325°F. Rinse blueberries, remove any stems, and drain. Place slightly damp blueberries in a bowl filled with powdered sugar and gently toss to coat. In a large bowl, combine flour, ½ cup powdered sugar, baking powder, salt, nutmeg, and cinnamon and mix well. Add brown sugar, vanilla, and milk and mix well. Strain blueberries to remove excess sugar. Fold blueberries into batter.

Put twelve paper liners into a muffin tin. Spoon batter into liners equally. Bake muffins for 40 minutes.

NUTRITIONAL INFORMATION PER SERVING			
Calories	197		
Protein	3 g	Dietary fiber	1 g
Carbohydrate	46 g	Cholesterol	0 mg
Fat	less than .5 g	Sodium	110 mg
% Calories from fat	2%		

MAPLE-AND-CORN MUFFINS

♦

Make sure you use real maple syrup in these delicious, sweet corn muffins.

12 SERVINGS / 1 MUFFIN PER SERVING

1½ cups flour
½ cup cornmeal
2 teaspoons baking powder
1 teaspoon salt
½ cup sugar

1 teaspoon vanilla extract
¼ cup fat-free egg substitute
  or 2 egg whites
1 cup skim milk
½ cup pure maple syrup

Preheat oven to 325°F. Combine flour, cornmeal, baking powder, and salt in a medium-sized bowl and mix well. In a large bowl, combine sugar, vanilla, egg substitute, milk, and maple syrup and mix well. Add dry mixture to wet mixture and mix well.

Put twelve paper liners into a muffin tin. Spoon batter into liners equally. Bake muffins for 30 minutes.

NUTRITIONAL INFORMATION PER SERVING			
Calories	151		
Protein	3 g	Dietary fiber	1 g
Carbohydrate	34 g	Cholesterol	0 mg
Fat	less than .5 g	Sodium	201 mg
% Calories from fat	2%		

APRICOT MUFFINS

These muffins are also tasty with a few chopped, toasted almonds mixed in. See the Index for chart that tells what this would add to the fat and calorie content per muffin.

12 SERVINGS / 1 MUFFIN PER SERVING

2 6-ounce packages dried
  apricots
1½ cups water
2 tablespoons light corn syrup
1 cup light brown sugar
¼ cup fat-free egg substitute
  or 2 egg whites

1 teaspoon vanilla extract
1 teaspoon finely grated
  orange rind
2½ cups flour
1 teaspoon salt
1 teaspoon baking soda
1 teaspoon baking powder

Coarsely chop apricots. Put apricots and water into a medium-sized saucepan and cover. Over medium heat, bring to a simmer. Reduce heat and simmer for about 3 minutes. Remove from heat and cool completely, keeping pan covered.

Preheat oven to 300°F. Add corn syrup, brown sugar, egg substitute, vanilla, and orange rind to cooled apricots. In a large bowl, mix together flour, salt, baking soda, and baking powder. Add cooled apricot mixture to flour mixture and mix well. Put twelve paper liners into a muffin tin. Spoon batter into the liners equally. Bake for 55–60 minutes.

NUTRITIONAL INFORMATION PER SERVING			
Calories	246		
Protein	4 g	Dietary fiber	3 g
Carbohydrate	58 g	Cholesterol	0 mg
Fat	less than .5 g	Sodium	305 mg
% Calories from fat	1%		

Pumpkin Pie (recipe on pages 112–113) ▶

Butterscotch-Banana Muffins

12 SERVINGS / 1 MUFFIN PER SERVING

MUFFINS
3½ cups flour
1½ teaspoons baking powder
1 teaspoon baking soda
1 teaspoon salt
2 very ripe medium-sized bananas
1 teaspoon vanilla extract
1 teaspoon rum extract
1½ cups sugar
½ cup fat-free egg substitute or 4 egg
*   whites*
1 cup fat-free butterscotch sundae topping

ICING
1 cup powdered sugar
¼ cup fat-free butterscotch sundae topping
¼ cup nonfat sour cream

Preheat oven to 325°F. Combine flour, baking powder, baking soda, and salt in a medium-sized bowl and mix well. In a large bowl, mash bananas. Add vanilla, rum extract, sugar, egg substitute, and butterscotch topping and mix well. Add dry mixture to banana mixture and mix well. Put twelve paper liners into a muffin tin. Spoon batter into liners equally. Bake muffins for 35 minutes.

After muffins have cooled, combine icing ingredients and mix well. Drizzle icing over the muffins.

NUTRITIONAL INFORMATION PER SERVING			
Calories	389		
Protein	5 g	Dietary fiber	1 g
Carbohydrate	91 g	Cholesterol	0 mg
Fat	less than .5 g	Sodium	365 mg
% Calories from fat	1%		

RAISIN BRAN MUFFINS

12 SERVINGS / 1 MUFFIN PER SERVING

1½ cups skim milk
1½ cups shredded bran cereal
1 cup raisins
1½ cups flour
1 teaspoon baking powder
½ teaspoon salt
1 cup sugar
½ cup skim milk
2 teaspoons vanilla extract
¼ cup fat-free egg substitute or *2 egg whites*
¼ cup molasses

Heat 1½ cups milk until just before it boils. Put cereal and raisins into a large bowl. Pour milk over and stir. In a medium-sized bowl, combine flour, baking powder, salt, and sugar and mix well. Add dry mixture to cereal mixture and mix well. Add ½ cup milk, vanilla, egg substitute, and molasses and mix well. Let batter sit for 30–60 minutes.

Preheat oven to 325°F. Put twelve paper liners into a muffin tin. Spoon batter into the liners equally. Bake muffins for 35 minutes.

NUTRITIONAL INFORMATION PER SERVING			
Calories	213		
Protein	5 g	Dietary fiber	4 g
Carbohydrate	51 g	Cholesterol	less than 1 mg
Fat	less than .5 g	Sodium	193 mg
% Calories from fat	2%		

Aunt Ouida's Cranberry Bread (recipe on pages 120–121) ▶

LEMON-RASPBERRY SURPRISE MUFFINS

These moist muffins have a great lemon flavor, a raspberry filling, and crumb topping.

12 SERVINGS / 1 MUFFIN PER SERVING

MUFFINS
2 cups flour
¾ teaspoon baking powder
½ teaspoon salt
1 3-ounce box cook-and-serve lemon
    pudding mix
1½ cups sugar
1 teaspoon vanilla extract
½ teaspoon lemon extract
¾ cup skim milk
4 ounces seedless raspberry jam (⅓ cup)

CRUMB TOPPING
¼ cup flour
¼ cup sugar
Pinch of salt
2–3 teaspoons seedless raspberry jam

Preheat oven to 325°F. In a small bowl, combine flour, baking powder, and salt and mix well. In a large bowl, combine pudding mix, sugar, vanilla, lemon extract, and milk and mix well. Add dry mixture to pudding mixture and mix well.

Put twelve paper liners into a muffin tin. Spoon batter into liners to fill about halfway. Spoon 1–1½ teaspoons of jam onto the center of the batter in each cup. Cover jam in each cup with remaining batter. Bake for 30 minutes.

Meanwhile, combine topping ingredients and mix to make crumbs. After muffins have baked for 30 minutes, remove tin from oven. Place a handful of crumb topping on each. Spread crumbs gently. Return muffins to oven and bake an additional 15–20 minutes.

NUTRITIONAL INFORMATION PER SERVING			
Calories	256		
Protein	3 g	Dietary fiber	.5 g
Carbohydrate	61 g	Cholesterol	0 mg
Fat	less than .5 g	Sodium	143 mg
% Calories from fat	1%		

Fudge Crunch Cupcakes

12 SERVINGS; 1 CUPCAKE PER SERVING

CUPCAKES
1⅓ cups flour
¼ cup unsweetened cocoa
  powder
1 teaspoon baking powder
½ teaspoon salt
1 cup sugar
1 teaspoon vanilla extract
1¼ cups skim milk
1–1⅓ cups miniature
  marshmallows

COCOA CRUNCH
  TOPPING
⅔ cup light brown sugar
⅓ cup flour
2 tablespoons unsweetened
  cocoa powder
1 teaspoon vanilla extract
¼ teaspoon salt
1 tablespoon skim milk

Preheat oven to 325°F. Combine flour, cocoa, baking powder, and salt in a medium-sized bowl and mix well. In a large bowl, combine sugar, vanilla, and milk and mix well. Add dry mixture to wet mixture and mix well. Put twelve paper liners into a muffin tin. Spoon batter into liners equally. Cover batter in each liner with about eight marshmallows and dunk them in the batter.

Combine topping ingredients and mix to make crumbs. Sprinkle crumbs over marshmallows. Bake cupcakes for 25 minutes.

NUTRITIONAL INFORMATION PER SERVING			
Calories	210		
Protein	3.5 g	Dietary fiber	1 g
Carbohydrate	48 g	Cholesterol	0 mg
Fat	less than .5 g	Sodium	156 mg
% Calories from fat	2%		

CHERRY CUPCAKES

12 SERVINGS; 1 CUPCAKE PER SERVING

CUPCAKES

2 cups flour

1½ teaspoons baking soda

½ teaspoon salt

½ teaspoon almond extract

1½ cups sugar

1 teaspoon vanilla extract

½ cup fat-free egg substitute
   or 4 egg whites

½ cup nonfat sour cream

1 21-ounce can cherry pie
   filling

ICING

¾ cup powdered sugar

¼ cup nonfat sour cream

⅛ teaspoon almond extract

Preheat oven to 325°F. Combine flour, baking soda, and salt in a medium-sized bowl and mix well. In a large bowl, combine almond extract, sugar, vanilla, egg substitute, and sour cream. Add dry mixture to wet mixture and mix well. Stir in pie filling.

Put twelve paper liners into a muffin tin. Spoon batter into liners equally. Bake cupcakes for 35 minutes.

After cupcakes have cooled, combine icing ingredients and mix well. Drizzle icing evenly over cupcakes.

NUTRITIONAL INFORMATION PER SERVING			
Calories	279		
Protein	3.5 g	Dietary fiber	1 g
Carbohydrate	66 g	Cholesterol	0 mg
Fat	less than .5 g	Sodium	286 mg
% Calories from fat	1%		

APPLE BREAKFAST CAKE

Topped with thinly sliced apples and cinnamon sugar, this is a delightful cake to serve at breakfast time.

8 SERVINGS

Butter-flavored cooking spray
1 cup flour
½ teaspoon baking powder
¼ teaspoon salt
¼ cup fat-free margarine
¼ cup light corn syrup
½ cup sugar
1 teaspoon vanilla extract
¼ cup fat-free egg substitute or 2 egg
  whites
2 Granny Smith apples
5 tablespoons sugar
1 teaspoon cinnamon

Preheat oven to 325°F. Spray base of a 10-inch springform pan with cooking spray and spread cooking spray with a paper towel. Cover base with waxed paper. Attach sides of pan. Use scissors to trim off excess waxed paper. Spray waxed paper and sides of pan with cooking spray and wipe with a paper towel to spread cooking spray evenly and absorb the excess.

In a small bowl, combine flour, baking powder, and salt and mix well. In a large bowl, combine margarine, corn syrup, ½ cup sugar, vanilla, and egg substitute and mix well. Add dry mixture to the wet mixture and mix well. Spread batter evenly over bottom of prepared pan.

Peel and core apples and slice thin. Arrange apples in a

pinwheel pattern on batter. Mix 5 tablespoons sugar with cinnamon and sprinkle over apples. Bake for 35–40 minutes. Cool for 10 minutes. Remove sides of pan and slide cake and waxed paper onto a serving plate. After cake cools completely, peel waxed paper off cake.

NUTRITIONAL INFORMATION PER SERVING			
Calories	200		
Protein	2 g	Dietary fiber	1 g
Carbohydrate	48 g	Cholesterol	0 mg
Fat	less than .5 g	Sodium	131 mg
% Calories from fat	1%		

RASPBERRY–CREAM CHEESE COFFEE CAKE

If you'd like, sprinkle a few almond slices with the crumb mixture over the top of this incredible coffee cake. See Index for chart that tells what this would add to the calorie and fat content per serving.

10 SERVINGS

Butter-flavored cooking spray
Flour to coat pan
2¼ cups flour
1 cup sugar
1 teaspoon salt
¼ cup fat-free margarine
½ teaspoon baking powder
½ teaspoon baking soda
½ teaspoon vanilla extract
½ teaspoon almond extract
1 cup nonfat sour cream
¼ cup skim milk
¼ cup fat-free egg substitute or 2 egg
  whites
16 ounces plain nonfat yogurt, drained
  (see Index)
½ cup sugar
¼ cup fat-free egg substitute or 2 egg
  whites
½ cup seedless raspberry jam

Preheat oven to 325°F. Spray base of a 10-inch springform pan with cooking spray and wipe with a paper towel. Cover the base with waxed paper. Attach sides of pan. Use scissors to trim off excess waxed paper. Spray waxed paper and sides of pan with cooking spray and wipe with a paper towel to spread cooking spray evenly and absorb the excess. Dust pan with flour and shake out the excess.

In a small bowl, combine 2¼ cups flour, 1 cup sugar, and salt and mix well. Blend in margarine until crumbly. Separate and reserve 1 cup of crumbs. To remaining crumb mixture, add baking powder, baking soda, vanilla, almond extract, sour cream, milk, and ¼ cup egg substitute and mix well. Batter may be slightly lumpy. Spread batter evenly over bottom of prepared pan.

In a small bowl, combine drained yogurt, ½ cup sugar, and ¼ cup egg substitute and mix well. Spread yogurt mixture over batter evenly. Carefully spoon jam over yogurt mixture evenly. Bake for 30 minutes.

Remove coffee cake from oven and sprinkle with reserved crumb mixture. Return coffee cake to oven and bake for an additional 25 minutes. Cool for about 10 minutes. Remove sides of pan and slide cake and waxed paper onto a serving plate. After cake cools completely, peel waxed paper off cake.

NUTRITIONAL INFORMATION PER SERVING			
Calories	314		
Protein	7 g	Dietary fiber	1 g
Carbohydrate	70 g	Cholesterol	1 mg
Fat	less than .5 g	Sodium	388 mg
% Calories from fat	1%		

CINNAMON-RAISIN COFFEE CAKE

This was one of the most popular coffee cakes with my taste-testing panel. It has a rich cinnamon-raisin filling and a cinnamon swirl on top that make it quite delicious and attractive.

12 SERVINGS

COFFEE CAKE
Butter-flavored cooking spray
3 cups flour
1 teaspoon baking soda
1 teaspoon baking powder
1 teaspoon salt
½ cup fat-free egg substitute or 4 egg
   whites
2 cups sugar
1½ cups nonfat sour cream
2 teaspoons vanilla extract

FILLING/TOPPING
1 cup light brown sugar
2 tablespoons flour
2 teaspoons cinnamon
⅛ teaspoon salt
2 tablespoons fat-free margarine
1 tablespoon plain nonfat yogurt
2 cups raisins

Preheat oven to 325°F. Spray a 13″ × 9″ pan with cooking spray and wipe with a paper towel to spread cooking spray evenly and absorb the excess. In a medium-sized bowl, mix together flour, baking soda, baking powder, and salt. In a large bowl, combine egg substitute, sugar, sour cream, and vanilla and mix well. Add dry mixture to wet mixture and mix well. Spread one-half of batter evenly over bottom of pan.

In a small bowl, combine all filling/topping ingredients except raisins and mix well. Spread one-half of filling/topping over batter in pan. Sprinkle raisins over filling. Spoon remaining batter over filling and raisins and spread evenly. Spoon remaining filling/topping on top and swirl with a fork or spoon. Bake for 40 minutes. Cool before serving.

NUTRITIONAL INFORMATION PER SERVING			
Calories	429		
Protein	6 g	Dietary fiber	2 g
Carbohydrate	101 g	Cholesterol	0 mg
Fat	less than .5 g	Sodium	387 mg
% Calories from fat	1%		

FRUIT-AND-CRUMB COFFEE CAKE

Make this with your favorite jam or preserves for a tasty treat at breakfast or snack time.

15 SERVINGS

Butter-flavored cooking spray
2½ cups flour
1 teaspoon baking powder
1 teaspoon cinnamon
1 teaspoon nutmeg
½ teaspoon salt
1 cup light brown sugar
¼ cup fat-free egg substitute or 2 egg
    whites
1¼ cups nonfat buttermilk
2 teaspoons vanilla extract
1 cup jam or preserves
1 cup flour
⅛ teaspoon salt
½ cup light brown sugar
2½ tablespoons plain nonfat yogurt

Preheat oven to 325°F. Spray a 13" × 9" pan with cooking spray and wipe with a paper towel to spread cooking spray evenly and absorb the excess.

In a large bowl, mix together 2½ cups flour, baking powder, cinnamon, nutmeg, ½ teaspoon salt, and 1 cup brown sugar. Add egg substitute, buttermilk, and vanilla and mix well. Spread batter in pan evenly. Spoon jam over batter in thick stripes and swirl with a fork or spoon. Bake for 25 minutes.

Meanwhile, combine 1 cup flour, ⅛ teaspoon salt, ½ cup

brown sugar, and yogurt in a medium-sized bowl and mix until crumbly. After coffee cake has baked 25 minutes, remove from oven and sprinkle with crumb mixture. Return coffee cake to oven and bake for an additional 5 minutes. Allow cake to cool before serving.

NUTRITIONAL INFORMATION PER SERVING			
Calories	261		
Protein	4 g	Dietary fiber	1 g
Carbohydrate	60 g	Cholesterol	0 mg
Fat	less than .5 g	Sodium	130 mg
% Calories from fat	2%		

7

Other Desserts

TROPICAL NUTMEG TRIFLE

This is a great summertime dessert that you can make with your favorite tropical fruits. I recommend a combination of bananas and pineapple. If you'd like, sprinkle some toasted coconut over the top. See Index for chart that tells what this would add to the fat and calorie content per serving.

18 SERVINGS

FILLING/TOPPING
16 ounces plain nonfat yogurt
½ teaspoon coconut extract
1 cup powdered sugar
4 tablespoons pineapple juice
40 large marshmallows
¼ cup skim milk

CAKE
Butter-flavored cooking spray
¾ cup sugar
¾ cup light brown sugar
1 teaspoon vanilla extract
¼ cup fat-free egg substitute or 2 egg
    whites
1¼ cups nonfat buttermilk
2 cups flour
½ teaspoon salt
1 tablespoon nutmeg
½ teaspoon baking powder
3–5 cups fresh fruit (pineapple chunks,
    berries, kiwi slices, banana slices, peach
    slices, etc.)

Combine yogurt, coconut extract, powdered sugar, and pineapple juice in a large bowl and mix well. In a medium-sized saucepan, melt marshmallows in milk over low heat, stirring frequently. Add melted marshmallows to yogurt mixture and mix well. Refrigerate.

Meanwhile, preheat oven to 325°F. Spray a 13" × 9" pan with cooking spray and wipe with a paper towel to absorb the excess. Combine sugar, brown sugar, vanilla, egg substitute, and buttermilk in a large bowl and mix well. Mix together flour, salt, nutmeg, and baking powder in a medium-sized bowl. Add dry mixture to wet mixture and mix well. Pour batter into pan. Bake for 30 minutes. When cake has cooled, cut into thirds.

Cut one-third of cake into 1"–2" cubes. Cover bottom of a large casserole dish with cubes. Top cubes with one-third of fresh fruit. Spoon one-third of refrigerated filling over fruit. Repeat these steps twice to complete assembly of trifle.

NUTRITIONAL INFORMATION PER SERVING			
Calories	245		
Protein	4.5 g	Dietary fiber	less than 1 g
Carbohydrate	57 g	Cholesterol	less than 1 mg
Fat	less than .5 g	Sodium	113 mg
% Calories from fat	2%		

Strawberry-Kiwi Cloud

This creamy dessert is full of fresh summer fruit and the zest of orange.

8 SERVINGS

16 ounces plain nonfat
  yogurt, drained (see Index)
1 cup nonfat sour cream
¼ teaspoon salt
1 teaspoon vanilla extract
3 tablespoons light corn syrup
1 cup nonfat dry milk powder

3 tablespoons cornstarch
¾ cup skim milk
1 cup sugar
Rind of 1 orange, grated fine
3 kiwi fruit, peeled and sliced
1 pint strawberries, sliced

Combine drained yogurt, sour cream, salt, vanilla, corn syrup, and milk powder in a large bowl and mix well. In a medium-sized saucepan, mix cornstarch with milk. Add sugar and orange rind to milk mixture and bring to a boil over medium heat, stirring constantly. Boil, stirring constantly, for about 1 minute. Add mixture in saucepan to mixture in large bowl and mix well.

Cool for about 2 hours. Stir in sliced kiwi fruit and strawberries. Spoon into eight serving dishes and chill completely.

NUTRITIONAL INFORMATION PER SERVING			
Calories	254		
Protein	8 g	Dietary fiber	1.5 g
Carbohydrate	55 g	Cholesterol	3 mg
Fat	less than .5 g	Sodium	198 mg
% Calories from fat	1%		

FUDGE BROWNIE PUDDING

With a fudge pudding base and a fudge brownie on top, this is a very rich dessert that can be served warm or cold. It's great plain or with a scoop of low-fat vanilla or pralines-and-cream ice cream on top.

12 SERVINGS

¾ cup sugar

1 cup flour

3 tablespoons unsweetened
  cocoa powder

1 teaspoon baking powder

¼ teaspoon salt

½ cup skim milk

1½ teaspoons vanilla extract

⅓ cup light corn syrup

½ cup sugar

½ cup light brown sugar

4 tablespoons unsweetened
  cocoa powder

1 tablespoon cornstarch

Pinch of salt

1¼ cups hot skim milk

Preheat oven to 325°F. Mix together ¾ cup sugar, flour, 3 tablespoons cocoa, baking powder, ¼ teaspoon salt, ½ cup milk, vanilla, and corn syrup. Pour batter into an 8-inch square baking pan.

Combine ½ cup sugar, brown sugar, 4 tablespoons cocoa, cornstarch, and pinch of salt and mix well. Sprinkle dry mixture evenly over batter. Pour hot milk over top of dry mixture. *Do not stir!* Bake for 35–40 minutes.

NUTRITIONAL INFORMATION PER SERVING			
Calories	211		
Protein	3 g	Dietary fiber	1 g
Carbohydrate	49 g	Cholesterol	less than 1 mg
Fat	less than .5 g	Sodium	84 mg
% Calories from fat	2%		

CHOCOLATE PUDDING

A B O U T 5 C U P S ; 1 0 S E R V I N G S
¹/₂ C U P P E R S E R V I N G

6 tablespoons cornstarch
4 cups skim milk
2 cups sugar
⅓ cup unsweetened cocoa powder
½ teaspoon salt
4 teaspoons vanilla extract

In medium-sized saucepan, dissolve cornstarch in ½ cup of the milk. Add remaining milk and stir well. Add sugar, cocoa, and salt. Cook over low heat, stirring continuously, until sugar is melted. Cook over medium heat, stirring continuously, until mixture begins to boil. Reduce heat and simmer, stirring continuously, for about 1 minute. Remove from heat and stir in vanilla.

Cool pudding uncovered in the refrigerator, stirring occasionally, until mixture is completely chilled. Spoon into ten serving dishes.

NUTRITIONAL INFORMATION PER SERVING			
Calories	222		
Protein	4 g	Dietary fiber	1 g
Carbohydrate	51 g	Cholesterol	1.6 mg
Fat	less than .5 g	Sodium	158 mg
% Calories from fat	2%		

POUND CAKE 'N' PUDDING

18 SERVINGS

Pound Cake (see Index)
Chocolate Pudding (see Index)

Make Pound Cake. Cut it into thirds, cover, and set aside.

Make Chocolate Pudding, but do not spoon it into dessert dishes.

To assemble dessert, cut one one-third section of pound cake into 1"–2" cubes. Cover bottom of a 2-quart casserole dish with cake cubes. Cover cubes with one-third of the pudding. Cut another one-third section of pound cake into cubes, layer cubes in casserole dish, cover cubes with one-third of the pudding, and repeat.

NUTRITIONAL INFORMATION PER SERVING			
Calories	337		
Protein	5.5 g	Dietary fiber	1 g
Carbohydrate	78 g	Cholesterol	1 mg
Fat	less than .5 g	Sodium	283 mg
% Calories from fat	1%		

BREAD PUDDING

Special thanks to Erica and Rance Smith and Virginia Frueh, who shared their bread pudding expertise with me. Also, thanks to an anonymous taste-tester who suggested that this would be great served with a lemon sauce. See Index for the lemon sauce I created with this good idea in mind.

9 SERVINGS

Butter-flavored cooking spray
10 slices light white bread, stale (8 ounces)
½ cup raisins
3 cups skim milk
1 cup sugar
½ cup light brown sugar
⅛ teaspoon salt
2 teaspoons vanilla extract
2 tablespoons flour
2 tablespoons fat-free margarine
¾ cup fat-free egg substitute or 6 egg whites

Preheat oven to 325°F. Spray a 2-quart glass casserole dish with cooking spray and wipe with a paper towel to spread cooking spray evenly and absorb the excess. Tear bread into small pieces and put in casserole dish. Add raisins.

Scald milk in a covered pan over low to medium heat and set aside. In a large bowl, combine remaining ingredients and mix well. Add scalded milk and mix well. Pour mixture over bread and raisins in casserole dish. Use a large spoon to press bread gently to make sure it is completely soaked. Bake for 45–50 minutes.

Cool for 15–20 minutes. Cover bread pudding with foil and cool completely.

NUTRITIONAL INFORMATION PER SERVING			
Calories	249		
Protein	7 g	Dietary fiber	1.5 g
Carbohydrate	57 g	Cholesterol	1.3 mg
Fat	less than .5 g	Sodium	237 mg
% Calories from fat	2%		

TRADITIONAL CHEESECAKE

♠

Cheesecakes are one of my favorite desserts, so I created five different fat-free cheesecake recipes. You'll be amazed that yogurt can taste like this! Try the topping called for below, or garnish with your favorite berries.

10 SERVINGS

CRUST
Butter-flavored cooking spray
30 fat-free wheat crackers
1¼ cups powdered sugar
½ cup plain nonfat yogurt

FILLING
32 ounces plain nonfat yogurt, drained
   (see Index)
2 cups sugar
3 tablespoons cornstarch
1 tablespoon lemon juice
2 teaspoons vanilla extract
½ cup fat-free egg substitute or 4 egg
   whites

TOPPING
1 cup nonfat sour cream
⅔ cup fruit preserves

Preheat oven to 300°F. Spray base of a 10-inch springform pan with cooking spray and wipe with a paper towel. Cover the base with waxed paper. Attach sides of pan. Use scissors to trim off excess waxed paper. Spray waxed paper and sides of pan with cooking spray and wipe with a paper towel to spread cooking spray evenly and absorb the excess.

Process crackers to make crumbs. Combine crumbs, powdered sugar, and yogurt. Press into bottom of pan (not up the side).

Combine filling ingredients and mix well. Pour filling over crust. Bake for 40 minutes. Cool cheesecake for about 5 minutes before removing sides of pan. Remove sides and cool completely.

Combine topping ingredients and mix well. Spread topping over cheesecake.

NUTRITIONAL INFORMATION PER SERVING			
Calories	389		
Protein	8.5 g	Dietary fiber	.5 g
Carbohydrate	89 g	Cholesterol	2 mg
Fat	less than .5 g	Sodium	197 mg
% Calories from fat	0%		

Chocolate Cheesecake

10 SERVINGS

CRUST
Butter-flavored cooking spray
30 fat-free wheat crackers
1¼ cups powdered sugar
½ cup plain nonfat yogurt

FILLING
32 ounces plain nonfat yogurt, drained
  (see Index)
2 cups sugar
½ cup unsweetened cocoa powder
1 tablespoon cornstarch
1 tablespoon skim milk
1 tablespoon vanilla extract
½ cup fat-free egg substitute or 4 egg
  whites

TOPPING
1 tablespoon fat-free margarine
1 tablespoon skim milk
½ tablespoon unsweetened cocoa powder
1 cup powdered sugar

Preheat oven to 300°F. Spray base of a 10-inch springform pan with cooking spray and wipe with a paper towel. Cover the base of pan with waxed paper. Attach sides of pan. Use scissors to trim off excess waxed paper. Spray waxed paper and sides of pan with cooking spray and wipe with a paper towel to spread cooking spray evenly and absorb the excess.

Process crackers to make crumbs. Combine crumbs, powdered

sugar, and yogurt. Press into bottom of pan (not up the side).

Combine filling ingredients and mix well. Pour filling over crust. Bake for 40 minutes. Cool cheesecake for about 5 minutes before removing sides of pan. Remove sides and cool completely.

Combine topping ingredients and mix well. Spread topping over cheesecake.

NUTRITIONAL INFORMATION PER SERVING			
Calories	368		
Protein	9 g	Dietary fiber	1.5 g
Carbohydrate	83 g	Cholesterol	2 mg
Fat	less than .5 g	Sodium	174 mg
% Calories from fat	1%		

AMARETTO CHEESECAKE

10 SERVINGS

CRUST
Butter-flavored cooking spray
30 fat-free wheat crackers
1¼ cups powdered sugar
½ cup plain nonfat yogurt

FILLING
32 ounces plain nonfat yogurt, drained
  (see Index)
2 cups sugar
3 tablespoons cornstarch
1 tablespoon amaretto (almond liqueur)
1 teaspoon vanilla extract
1 teaspoon almond extract
½ cup fat-free egg substitute or 4 egg
  whites

TOPPING
1½ cups nonfat sour cream
½ cup sugar
1 teaspoon almond extract
2 teaspoons chopped almonds, toasted

Preheat oven to 300°F. Spray base of a 10-inch springform pan with cooking spray and wipe with a paper towel. Cover the base of pan with waxed paper. Attach sides of pan. Use scissors to trim off excess waxed paper. Spray waxed paper and sides of pan with cooking spray and wipe with a paper towel to spread cooking spray evenly and absorb the excess.

Process crackers to make crumbs. Combine crumbs, powdered

sugar, and yogurt. Press into bottom of pan (not up the side).

Combine filling ingredients and mix well. Pour filling over crust. Bake for 40 minutes. Cool cheesecake for about 5 minutes before removing sides of pan. Remove sides and cool completely.

Combine topping ingredients and mix well. Spread topping over cheesecake.

NUTRITIONAL INFORMATION PER SERVING			
Calories	389		
Protein	9 g	Dietary fiber	.5 g
Carbohydrate	86 g	Cholesterol	2 mg
Fat	less than .5 g	Sodium	210 mg
Alcohol	1.3 g		
% Calories from fat	1%		

Coconut–Fudge Swirl Cheesecake

10 SERVINGS

CRUST
Butter-flavored cooking spray
30 fat-free wheat crackers
1¼ cups powdered sugar
½ cup plain nonfat yogurt

FILLING
32 ounces plain nonfat yogurt, drained
  (see Index)
2 cups sugar
3 tablespoons cornstarch
1 tablespoon skim milk
1 teaspoon vanilla extract
1 teaspoon coconut extract
½ cup fat-free egg substitute or 4 egg
  whites
3 tablespoons unsweetened cocoa powder
1 tablespoon flaked coconut

Preheat oven to 300°F. Spray base of a 10-inch springform pan with cooking spray and wipe with a paper towel. Cover base of pan with waxed paper. Attach sides of pan. Use scissors to trim off excess waxed paper. Spray waxed paper and sides of pan with cooking spray and wipe with a paper towel to spread cooking spray evenly and absorb the excess.

    Process crackers to make crumbs. Combine crumbs, powdered sugar, and yogurt. Press into bottom of pan (not up the side).

    Combine all filling ingredients except cocoa and coconut and mix well. Remove 1 cup of filling mixture and mix with cocoa. Add coconut to remaining filling. Pour coconut filling over crust.

Place spoonfuls of cocoa mixture over coconut filling in pan and use a fork to swirl. Bake for 40 minutes. Cool cheesecake for about 5 minutes before removing sides of pan. Cool completely.

NUTRITIONAL INFORMATION PER SERVING			
Calories	316		
Protein	8 g	Dietary fiber	1 g
Carbohydrate	71 g	Cholesterol	2 mg
Fat	less than .5 g	Sodium	163 mg
% Calories from fat	1%		

PRALINE CHEESECAKE

10 SERVINGS

CRUST
Butter-flavored cooking spray
30 fat-free wheat crackers
1¼ cups powdered sugar
½ cup plain nonfat yogurt

FILLING
32 ounces plain nonfat yogurt, drained
  (see Index)
1½ cups light brown sugar
4 tablespoons cornstarch
2 tablespoons pecan liqueur
½ cup fat-free egg substitute or 4 egg
  whites

TOPPING
1½ cups nonfat sour cream
⅓ cup light brown sugar
1 teaspoon pecan liqueur
½ tablespoon finely chopped pecans

Preheat oven to 300°F. Spray base of a 10-inch springform pan with cooking spray and wipe with a paper towel. Cover base of pan with waxed paper. Attach sides of pan. Use scissors to trim off excess waxed paper. Spray waxed paper and sides of pan with cooking spray and wipe with a paper towel to spread cooking spray evenly and absorb the excess.

Process crackers to make crumbs. Combine crumbs, powdered sugar, and yogurt. Press into bottom of pan (not up the side).

Combine filling ingredients and mix well. Pour filling over

crust. Bake for 50 minutes. Cool cheesecake for about 5 minutes before removing sides of pan. Remove sides and cool completely.

Combine topping ingredients and mix well. Spread topping over cheesecake.

NUTRITIONAL INFORMATION PER SERVING			
Calories	354		
Protein	9 g	Dietary fiber	.5 g
Carbohydrate	77 g	Cholesterol	2 mg
Fat	less than .5 g	Sodium	225 mg
Alcohol	1.4 g		
% Calories from fat	1%		

BUCKEYE INSPIRATIONS

Many thanks to my husband's grandmother, Virginia Frueh, for providing the inspiration for this recipe. Actually, it was the raves I'd heard about her buckeyes that inspired me to ask for the original recipe and attempt to create my own version. These are not meant to be an equivalent, but a variant. Whether these taste like buckeyes is debatable, but they were certainly a big hit with my taste-testing panel.

ABOUT 80; 40 SERVINGS/2 PER SERVING

FILLING
1 4.5-ounce box fat-free sugar cones
75 fat-free wheat crackers
¼ cup fat-free margarine
½ cup skim milk
4 cups powdered sugar
1 tablespoon vanilla extract
2 tablespoons reduced-fat peanut butter

CHOCOLATE COATING
4 tablespoons unsweetened cocoa powder
2 cups powdered sugar
⅛ teaspoon salt
½ teaspoon vanilla extract
⅓ cup plus 1–2 tablespoons skim milk

Use a food processor to make crumbs from cones and crackers. Combine margarine, milk, powdered sugar, vanilla, and peanut butter in a large bowl and mix well. Add the crumbs to the mixture in the large bowl and mix well. Use your hands to press filling into 1″–1¼″ balls.

Combine chocolate coating ingredients in a medium-sized

bowl and mix well. Dunk each filling ball in the chocolate coating and set on a sheet of foil to dry.

NUTRITIONAL INFORMATION PER SERVING			
Calories	114		
Protein	1.5 g	Dietary fiber	.5 g
Carbohydrate	26 g	Cholesterol	0 mg
Fat	less than .5 g	Sodium	92 mg
% Calories from fat	3%		

CHOCOLATE-COVERED STRAWBERRIES

10 SERVINGS/2-4 STRAWBERRIES PER SERVING, DEPENDING ON THEIR SIZE

1 quart strawberries
4 tablespoons unsweetened cocoa powder
2 cups powdered sugar
1/8 teaspoon salt
1/2 teaspoon vanilla extract
4 1/2 tablespoons skim milk

Rinse and dry strawberries; do not remove stems. In a medium-sized bowl, combine remaining ingredients and mix well. Dip each strawberry in the chocolate mixture and set on a plate. If there is extra chocolate, spoon over strawberries. Serve the same day.

NUTRITIONAL INFORMATION PER SERVING			
Calories	123		
Protein	1 g	Dietary fiber	1.5 g
Carbohydrate	30 g	Cholesterol	0 mg
Fat	less than .5 g	Sodium	31 mg
% Calories from fat	3%		

Maple-and-Corn Muffins (recipe on page 129) ▶

Blueberry Cobbler

9 SERVINGS

FILLING
Butter-flavored cooking spray
1 quart blueberries
⅔ cup sugar
1 teaspoon cinnamon
 (optional)
1 tablespoon lemon juice

TOPPING
1½ cups flour
½ teaspoon baking powder
½ teaspoon salt
¾ cup light brown sugar
¼ cup fat-free egg substitute
 or 2 egg whites
2 tablespoons fat-free
 margarine
½ cup skim milk
1 teaspoon vanilla extract

Preheat oven to 325°F. Spray an 11″ × 9″ × 2½″ roasting pan with cooking spray and wipe with a paper towel. Rinse blueberries and place them in pan. Sprinkle sugar, cinnamon, and lemon juice evenly over blueberries and stir.

In a medium-sized bowl, combine flour, baking powder, and salt and mix well. In a large bowl, combine brown sugar, egg substitute, margarine, milk, and vanilla and mix well. Add dry mixture to wet mixture and mix well. Pour batter evenly over blueberries in pan. Bake for 50 minutes. Serve warm or cold.

NUTRITIONAL INFORMATION PER SERVING			
Calories	250		
Protein	3.5 g	Dietary fiber	2 g
Carbohydrate	59 g	Cholesterol	0 mg
Fat	less than .5 g	Sodium	167 mg
% Calories from fat	2%		

CRANBERRY MOLD

8 SERVINGS

1 cup nonfat sour cream
1 7-ounce jar marshmallow creme
1 16-ounce can whole berry cranberry
   sauce
1 11-ounce can mandarin orange
   segments
1 envelope unflavored gelatin

In a large bowl, combine sour cream and marshmallow creme and mix well. Add cranberry sauce and mix well. In a small saucepan, stir together the liquid from orange segments and gelatin. Set orange segments aside. Let gelatin mixture sit for about 1 minute. Cook gelatin mixture over low heat until gelatin is completely dissolved. Add gelatin mixture to sour cream mixture and mix well. Stir in orange segments. Pour mixture into a ring mold and chill until firm.

NUTRITIONAL INFORMATION PER SERVING			
Calories	220		
Protein	2.5 g	Dietary fiber	1 g
Carbohydrate	52 g	Cholesterol	0 mg
Fat	less than .5 g	Sodium	71 mg
% Calories from fat	1%		

PINEAPPLE MOLD

8 SERVINGS

½ *cup water*
1 15¼-*ounce can crushed pineapple in its*
    own juice
1 3-*ounce package orange or orange-*
    pineapple flavor gelatin dessert mix
½ *teaspoon coconut extract*
16 *ounces plain nonfat yogurt, drained*
    (see Index)
2 *tablespoons flaked coconut*
2 *cups miniature marshmallows*

In a small saucepan, stir together water, the liquid from pineapple, and gelatin mix. Set pineapple aside. Let gelatin mixture sit for about 1 minute. Cook gelatin mixture over low heat until gelatin is completely dissolved. In a large bowl, combine gelatin mixture, coconut extract, and drained yogurt and mix well. Stir in pineapple, coconut, and marshmallows. Pour mixture into a ring mold and chill until firm.

NUTRITIONAL INFORMATION PER SERVING			
Calories	138		
Protein	4.5 g	Dietary fiber	.5 g
Carbohydrate	31 g	Cholesterol	1 mg
Fat	less than .5 g	Sodium	62 mg
% Calories from fat	3%		

Milk Chocolate Ice Cream

ABOUT 7 CUPS; 8 SERVINGS

A LITTLE LESS THAN 1 CUP PER SERVING

2 cups sugar
½ cup nonfat dry milk powder
¼ teaspoon salt
4 tablespoons cornstarch
2 tablespoons unsweetened cocoa powder
4 cups skim milk
1 12-ounce can evaporated skimmed milk
2 teaspoons vanilla extract

In a large saucepan, combine sugar, milk powder, salt, cornstarch, and cocoa and mix well. Add milk, evaporated milk, and vanilla and mix well. Cook over medium heat, stirring constantly, until mixture begins to boil. Reduce heat and simmer, stirring continuously for 5 minutes.

Remove pan from heat and cool uncovered. Chill completely in the refrigerator. Pour into an ice cream maker and follow manufacturer's instructions to make ice cream.

NUTRITIONAL INFORMATION PER SERVING			
Calories	313		
Protein	10 g	Dietary fiber	less than .5 g
Carbohydrate	68 g	Cholesterol	4 mg
Fat	less than .5 g	Sodium	210 Mg
% Calories from fat	1%		

Vanilla Bean Ice Cream

Vanilla beans are expensive, but the flavor they add is worth it!

ABOUT 7 CUPS; 8 SERVINGS

A LITTLE LESS THAN 1 CUP PER SERVING

2 cups skim milk
1 vanilla bean
2 cups skim milk
1 12-ounce can evaporated
   skimmed milk

2 cups sugar
½ cup nonfat dry milk powder
¼ teaspoon salt
4 tablespoons cornstarch

Put 2 cups of milk in a large saucepan. Cut the vanilla bean into 3–4 segments. Slice each segment in half lengthwise. Scrape seeds from bean. Add seeds and bean segments to milk in saucepan. Cover pan and cook over low heat for about 20 minutes. Make sure mixture does not boil hard or burn.

Remove pan from heat; remove bean segments. Add 2 cups milk and evaporated milk to pan. In a medium-sized bowl, combine sugar, milk powder, salt, and cornstarch and mix well. Add dry mixture to mixture in saucepan and mix well. Cook over medium heat, stirring constantly, until mixture begins to boil. Reduce heat and simmer, stirring continuously, for 5 minutes.

Remove pan from heat and cool uncovered. Chill completely in the refrigerator. Pour into an ice cream maker and follow manufacturer's instructions to make ice cream.

NUTRITIONAL INFORMATION PER SERVING			
Calories	304		
Protein	9 g	Dietary fiber	less than .5 g
Carbohydrate	67 g	Cholesterol	4 mg
Fat	less than .5 g	Sodium	210 mg
% Calories from fat	1%		

COFFEE ICE CREAM

ABOUT 7 CUPS; 8 SERVINGS

A LITTLE LESS THAN 1 CUP PER SERVING

2 cups sugar
½ cup nonfat dry milk powder
¼ teaspoon salt
4 tablespoons cornstarch
4–8 teaspoons instant coffee granules
4 cups skim milk
1 12-ounce can evaporated skimmed milk
2 teaspoons vanilla extract

In a large saucepan, combine sugar, milk powder, salt, cornstarch, and coffee and mix well. Add milk, evaporated milk, and vanilla and mix well. Cook over medium heat, stirring continuously, until mixture begins to boil. Reduce heat and simmer, stirring continuously for 5 minutes.

Remove pan from heat and cool uncovered. Chill completely in the refrigerator. Pour into an ice cream maker and follow manufacturer's instructions to make ice cream.

NUTRITIONAL INFORMATION PER SERVING			
Calories	310		
Protein	9 g	Dietary fiber	0 g
Carbohydrate	68 g	Cholesterol	4 mg
Fat	less than .5 g	Sodium	210 mg
% Calories from fat	1%		

TROPICAL FRUIT DIP

Serve this tasty dip with your favorite fresh fruit.

ABOUT 3½ CUPS; 14 SERVINGS
¼ CUP PER SERVING

1 3-ounce box cook-and-serve banana
   pudding mix
1 cup skim milk
¼ teaspoon coconut extract
1 cup nonfat sour cream
1 cup powdered sugar
1 8-ounce can crushed pineapple in syrup
3 tablespoons flaked coconut, toasted (see
   Index)

In a small saucepan, combine pudding mix and milk. Cook over medium heat, stirring continuously, until mixture begins to boil. Remove pan from heat. In a large bowl, combine pudding, coconut extract, sour cream, and powdered sugar and mix well. Stir in pineapple and coconut. Chill.

NUTRITIONAL INFORMATION PER SERVING			
Calories	96		
Protein	1 g	Dietary fiber	2 g
Carbohydrate	22 g	Cholesterol	0 mg
Fat	less than .5 g	Sodium	82 mg
% Calories from fat	4%		

Traditional Cheesecake (recipe on pages 158–159) ▶

LEMON SAUCE

This sauce is best served warm. Try spooning some over a serving of Bread Pudding (see Index).

ABOUT 3 CUPS; 9 SERVINGS
$^1/_3$ CUP PER SERVING

1 2.9-ounce box cook-and-serve lemon
   pudding mix
½ cup sugar
2¾ cups skim milk

In a medium-sized sauce pan, stir together pudding mix, sugar, and ¼ cup of the milk until all lumps are gone. Add 2 cups of the milk and cook over medium heat until mixture boils. Cool for 10 minutes. Add ½ cup of the milk and mix well.

NUTRITIONAL INFORMATION PER SERVING			
Calories	103		
Protein	2.5 g	Dietary fiber	0 g
Carbohydrate	23 g	Cholesterol	1.2 mg
Fat	less than .5 g	Sodium	85 mg
% Calories from fat	1%		

Hot Fudge Sauce

ABOUT 3 CUPS; 16 SERVINGS

3 TABLESPOONS PER SERVING

3 cups sugar

½ cup unsweetened cocoa powder

1½ cups skim milk

¼ teaspoon salt

2 tablespoons light corn syrup

2 tablespoons fat-free margarine

1 teaspoon vanilla extract

In a medium-sized saucepan, combine all ingredients except margarine and vanilla. Stir over low heat until sugar is melted. Over medium heat, continue to stir until mixture reaches a hard boil and begins to rise. Reduce heat and simmer, stirring continuously, for 5 minutes. Remove pan from heat and stir in margarine and vanilla. Cool uncovered. Warm in a microwave before serving.

NUTRITIONAL INFORMATION PER SERVING			
Calories	174		
Protein	1.5 g	Dietary fiber	.5 g
Carbohydrate	42 g	Cholesterol	0 mg
Fat	less than .5 g	Sodium	70 mg
% Calories from fat	2%		

Caramel Sauce

ABOUT 3 CUPS; 16 SERVINGS
3 TABLESPOONS PER SERVING

3 cups dark brown sugar
1½ cups skim milk
⅜ teaspoon salt
3 tablespoons fat-free margarine
3 teaspoons vanilla extract

Combine brown sugar, milk, and salt in a large saucepan and cook, stirring continuously, over low heat until sugar is melted. Bring to a hard boil over medium heat, stirring continuously. Mixture will begin to rise. Simmer, stirring continuously, for about 2 minutes. Remove from heat and add margarine, stirring until it dissolves. Add vanilla and stir. Cool completely.

NUTRITIONAL INFORMATION PER SERVING			
Calories	166		
Protein	less than 1 g	Dietary fiber	0 g
Carbohydrate	42 g	Cholesterol	0 mg
Fat	less than .5 g	Sodium	86 mg
% Calories from fat	0%		

Index

J.P.Morgan

RESILIENT

SEVETRI WILSON

RESILIENT

How to Overcome *ANYTHING*
& Build a Million Dollar Business
With or Without
Capital

WILEY

Published by John Wiley & Sons, Inc., Hoboken, New Jersey.
Published simultaneously in Canada.

For general information on our other products and services or for technical support, please contact our Customer Care Department within the United States at (800) 762-2974, outside the United States at (317) 572-3993 or fax (317) 572-4002.

Wiley publishes in a variety of print and electronic formats and by print-on-demand. Some material included with standard print versions of this book may not be included in e-books or in print-on-demand. If this book refers to media such as a CD or DVD that is not included in the version you purchased, you may download this material at http://booksupport.wiley.com. For more information about Wiley products, visit www.wiley.com.

Library of Congress Cataloging-in-Publication Data is available:

ISBN 9781119773870 (Hardcover)
ISBN 9781119774037 (ePDF)
ISBN 9781119773931 (ePub)

Cover design: Paul McCarthy
Cover image: © Getty Images | Baona

SKY10026537_042321

A special thank you to my tribe, support system, and everyone who continues to show up for me in unexpected ways. Thank you to Jeanenne for feeling that my startup and business story should be told.

Thank you to my Mama and Daddy, who taught me to be Resilient. Even in death, you continue to give me life.

This one is for all the aspiring entrepreneurs and the entrepreneurs who have faced the ups and downs of starting something. It's for the team members who have stayed on throughout the journey to build something special even amidst the unknown. It's for the resilient builder in all of us.

Contents

Introduction

You can't always be first, but you can be better.
—Sevetri Wilson

Before the coronavirus spread across the globe, we were just settling into a brand new office in New York City and positioning our executive team to grow from there—all while maintaining our office in New Orleans, which allowed me to keep my promise to cultivate talent from the place I'm from.

See, the year 2020 was supposed to be a big deal. But then as the agony began of watching, as many of my friends and family were laid off or saw their businesses shutter, I started to realize that 2020 was definitely not going to be what I had bargained for. Then as the year progressed and with the aftermath of the last several months, COVID-19, the murder of George Floyd and Breonna Taylor, as well as the protests across the world that would follow, 2020 was *still a big deal*! 2020 was a year of reckoning for many, forcing everyone to come to grips with the end of normalcy as we've known it. COVID-19 took with it jobs and security for hard-working families across the world. Here in the United States we were slow to respond, some even slower than others. On a call with an investor, we discussed how businesses would now be tested more than ever. Some of us would come out on top (those that were fortunate), some would stay flat (also fortunate), and others would close. The pandemic would test our ability to pivot or capture new opportunities, but more than anything it would test our sanity and ability to keep our teams going when everything around us was turned upside down.

This book is different. I hadn't imagined writing it while going through a pandemic and through our generation's version of a Civil Rights movement.

Yet, in this book I'm going to go there. I'm going to walk you through how I bootstrapped my first business to how I raised millions for my second company, all while retaining majority control; all while at the onset of a pandemic. My hope is that this book will offer something that was missing when I started building as an entrepreneur. I hope that it will shed light on what seems like the impossible, and bring new ways of thinking about challenges. I hope it is a bridge to the other side of your goals, a "how-to" guide of sorts that will bring about the awakening and push you've been looking for. I hope that it is both inspirational and aspirational. Never would I have imagined that someone like me, a first-generation college student who went to school on a full Pell grant, who grew up in a six-person household while her mother brought in a $26,000 yearly salary, would make it this far. There was no one to teach me the blueprint, but I hope to show you how I built my company from literally nothing while providing a ground-up approach, one where you can start from anywhere.

This book won't be an easy ride, but neither is business. Instead, I hope it will be a journey to economic and financial freedom through ownership, as that is what building a business has been for me.

1

Coming From Where I'm From

To be a woman you have to look like a girl, act like a lady, think like a man, and work like a dog.
—Leah Chase

Attending Louisiana State University (LSU) for undergrad opened up an entirely new world for me. I come from a small town about 45 minutes outside of New Orleans, the city where my mama and her family are from.

The first time I became really aware of technology was when I was in middle school, when my mother brought home our first computer, a Dell desktop. We didn't have the Internet, but my Mama would get these AOL dial-up cards for free. Now, obviously, I would be exposed more to technology in college, but I had no idea that my journey would lead me into tech.

At LSU, I met a professor who truly pushed me and many others to go beyond the thinking of the small towns we came from. Dr. Leonard Moore would likely have the single most impactful role in my life while I was in college—so much so that I added history as a second major. Yet, more than anything, he showed how someone could manage multiple opportunities. He had written books naturally as a college professor, but he and his wife Thais had also started a program for youth, and a youth church. He was living a life that I had never imagined was a possibility. There was nothing luxurious about it, either; outwardly at least he lived very modestly but I had never seen this coming from where I was from. Over the course of my life, exposure has helped me more than anything to actually realize the possibilities of not only my work, but what my life could be like as well.

Doc would say that if you do something you are passionate about, you don't watch the clock. These thoughts of how I could use what I was good at to build something I loved wouldn't die, so entrepreneurship for me started at a young age.

I went to a large university—a Southeastern Conference (SEC) school with over 30,000 students and a national title-winning football team, so we were one of the first colleges to have Facebook. The coolest thing about Facebook then besides another place to post with your friends was that you were able to upload albums and sell and buy furniture on their marketplace.

Yet, for the most part, people were still on Facebook without a face. Instagram wasn't really a thing. Twitter was just taking off, with celebrities posting about their projects or other tidbits about their day.

I created *B-NOW*, a college online newspaper, when I was in school, and my first company would come when I was 22.

I've never been afraid to start something on my own. I think this goes to having confidence in your ability to figure it out even if your capabilities aren't there yet. Yes, in a way you can fake it until you make it, but eventually you're going to really have to make it. But more so, this is about starting somewhere so that over time you can become an expert at what you do and command the type of payment you used to only wish for.

Even with that, I had a lot of hiccups along the way because I had to really grasp and understand not only how to run a business but how to start a business from nothing. I didn't inherit a business and I didn't have anyone to turn to show me the ropes.

There are a lot of challenges that you are faced with when starting, and then running, a business. It's still challenging, you know, even as a second-time business owner now building a company to scale.

As a business owner, you have key responsibilities to your team, to your clients, to your investors if you have them, to the IRS—you name it.

You have to ensure that your business is legally sound. You have to ensure that you are paying people correctly, whether they are a W-9 or W-2 employee. You have to decide when and if you want to go from W-9 employees to W-2 employees and know the differences between them. There is so much foundational work that goes into play in building a business, particularly one you plan to grow, that if you don't do certain things correctly they will come back to haunt you.

Then there is the actual work: going after contract opportunities, and building and selling whatever product or service you are offering to bring revenue into your company.

Most importantly, you have to make your business make sense. When you're trying to get people in the door or contracts closed you will feel the pressure to take what sticks or whatever someone is offering you. It will on first sight look like an opportunity, but could be anything but. I talk later about upside-down contracts. When you are venture-backed you might take on a customer where the financial gain might not be as rewarding but the benefits you receive from the deal, because of a prominent logo or other reason, might be worth it, whereas if you are bootstrapped this might be a luxury you can't afford.

As a bootstrapped company one thing you have to learn quickly is how to monetize what you are seeking to do. People know that one of my favorite things to remind entrepreneurs of is that you are in business to make money; otherwise, what you're doing is solely a passion project. What I've found is that the real magic happens when you can be both. If you prioritize one over the other you'll likely start to question yourself and whether it's worth it. Passionate about a business that doesn't make you money? You'll certainly suffer from fatigue and burnout, and eventually your business will most likely fold because you can't sustain a business that's not profitable.

Only in it for the money? The initial rush of having money will satisfy a part of you, but the longing for something more will without doubt catch up with you and that's a different type of fatigue and burnout in itself.

Triple Threat

As a business owner I was a "triple threat"—and not in a good way. I was Black, a woman, and young. And so, in many ways, when I was hitting roadblocks early on I felt the world was working against me. I had individuals across the table who weren't that much older than me, but they didn't look like me and so some of the struggles that come along with that were questioning myself, like oh man, what am I doing here again? Should I even be doing this or that?—the questions I was asking myself was a challenge within itself, and because there was no one else at the table who looked like me who was I suppose to ask were my feelings valid?

But I was here and I felt like I had nothing to lose, and I mean that very literally. My mother had just passed away when I graduated college and I started my company six months after that, and for me it was like, you know, I had spent so much time wanting to create this life so that I could help my mother, I felt like she'd missed out on so much and she had given so much to her children. When she passed away, I really had to rebuild in many ways.

I had to reframe what it was that I was living for. I'd launch my first business, Solid Ground Innovations (SGI), in July 2009, but wouldn't make it publicly known outside of my clients until 2011, which is also when I started to see real growth within the business.

I experienced so many lessons down the road, and it's important to know that you will face a lot of challenges. I made money. I lost money. I had contract deals that, starting out, I would have never dreamed of. I had an employee steal from the business by creating fake vendor invoices. I was furious. I had to fire my own clients because I no longer wanted to work within a situation that was not designed for anyone to succeed.

Yet, if it weren't for these hard lessons that I learned within SGI, I don't think I would have been as prepared to start a second company. Without the success of SGI, Resilia wouldn't exist today.

When you're first starting off in a business you feel like you can't turn down work, at least not paid work. I look back to some of those situations and today I wouldn't touch some of the work we took then because it wouldn't make sense. Time is one of my most valuable assets, and you don't want to waste it on deals that aren't worth it.

Choosing to turn down some work was one of the most refreshing moments in business for me. I was coming into my own as a business owner and leader; I could take opportunities that were meant for me and pass on the ones that I thought were not. But it wasn't always like this. Early on I had to build my capabilities, and create a name in the industry, and prove that we could compete, so I was happy to do work to build my portfolio and resume. This didn't mean working for free, but it did mean that the rate I charged in 2010 was a fraction of what I charge today.

I also made a conscious decision to stay in Louisiana and build my business where I was from. Not once but twice. People are always floored that I've made this decision, but I'd been committed to creating an ecosystem for minority business owners, and those who I never saw get a chance to sit at the table.

Building a business in the Deep South as a Black woman is challenging—and that is putting it lightly. At times, I thought maybe it wasn't meant for me to be here. Maybe I needed to go somewhere else because I could grow faster, I could hire from a larger talent pool. Eventually I would open up offices in other cities to create this dynamic, but I stick with my initial thoughts on if you leave at the moment you taste success, then you never grow an ecosystem where things do grow faster, where the pool of talent does become bigger where you're from. I also grappled with the idea that maybe I couldn't be a "king" on my own land—something I would paraphrase when talking to my mentor about the biblical saying "no one is a prophet in their own land." A lot of entrepreneurs may experience this phenomenon where they don't feel supported where they are from. The idea is that when people are too familiar with you they're not as attracted to you as they would be to someone they are less familiar with. This is also perhaps why you see statements like people support strangers before they support those they know. Even Jay-Z had a verse in his track "Boss" that said, "rather work for the man than to work for me." Yet, there were times where I was really frustrated. In many ways, I'm still frustrated. I had been on all the lists—the LSU 100 fastest-growing businesses, all the 40-under-40 lists in and out of my state; I had joined the most exclusive boards. I had helped people secure powerful roles and jobs, and when they were in a position to help me never lifted a finger. I had won a Pulitzer Prize for public service. I had been recognized by the White House. I checked off all the boxes. Why was it still so hard for me to access resources?

Maybe one of the reasons I'm still here is also so that I can extend support to other entrepreneurs, the support I felt it took me a very long time to receive. The support I feel like I still don't always receive.

When I started a tech company I knew I'd have to venture out of Louisiana if I wanted a chance at scale and to grow faster, and we now have a second office in New York City.

When I went out to raise capital for the first time, the journey was intense. I had never raised capital before, but surely once I showed investors how well my first company was doing and how I had bootstrapped it to seven figures and had already started to gain traction for Resilia, it would be a no-brainer. Right?

The idea of raising capital when I first started out in business wasn't even a factor. It just wasn't something you did where I was from. So, when I saw all of these headlines, with people more captivated with companies that had raised tens of millions of dollars, but not have the same enthusiasm or press attention for those who had *made* tens of millions of dollars, it was odd to me.

By the time I had closed my seed round I had made far more money in my first bootstrapped business than I had raised, but when news of my raising $2 million became public, it went viral. I was shocked. I wasn't on the tech scene. I was just in New Orleans building a company out of sight; so many people, especially within the realm of Black tech, had never heard of me, and because of this I seemed to have come out of nowhere. In reality, I had started my first venture almost a decade prior.

As a two-time founder, I know not to get caught up in the hype of it all. The way society moves today, they will crown you and then dethrone you in a New York minute. As the CEO and founder of a company, I start my day by literally just trying to get my mind right. On Sunday, I begin to prepare for my week ahead. I've found that going into Monday even a little more prepared than if I didn't do anything decreases anxiety. I know a lot of entrepreneurs and even individuals who have jobs and careers feel this on Sunday night, setting in right around 5 p.m. or so. A lot of entrepreneurs in general are like that when they're just coming up: they have anxiety on Sunday night because they know they're about to start the new week. For me it's definitely been one of those things where I'm very intentional in my thinking.

I started doing meditation and my friend Summer, and then another one of my friends, Jason introduced me to a guided meditation using Muse (a wearable brain-sensing headband). It helps me be very conscious of the energy I take in and give out. Most importantly it helps me focus and limit the normal distractions of the day—and how I move. It's about practicing mindfulness and trying yourself to let go negativity and calm your mind and body.

It's important for me to focus on what's in front of me and what's ahead of me. Entrepreneurship can be a lonely journey. You're going to be tested in many ways, especially if you are a minority. You really have to have the confidence to not be shaken, but even if your confidence *is* shaken, you can't let it break you.

If you're not confident, things will start chipping away at you little by little, and you start to realize that some of the issues you may be having really stem from the fact that you just lost your confidence somewhere along the way.

This can also potentially put you in a position of resentment or jade you in a way that you become a detriment not only to your own success but potentially to other people as well. That's why I believe that when women founders meet women investors or other women along the way who are harder on them than men, or treat them negatively, it's because of what they faced along their journey. No one should have to endure anything that makes them feel lesser than. So on the journey, be sure to treat others the way you would have wanted to be treated when you were in their position. Lift as you climb.

Because of experiences like this, I've been super mindful about ensuring that I connect with women, especially Black women, and being really intentional about how I can help within reason.

I felt that I was missing a lot of support. My father passed away when I was about 9, and then my mother passed away when I was 21, four days before Christmas. She had an aggressive form of cancer and within 3 months time she was no longer here. I was in grad school at the time and during her initial chemotherapy I drove the 50-minute trip every day to be with her at night. There is something about watching the person you love most wither away like she did that changes you forever.

The next year, after my mother passed, I went on to start Solid Ground Innovations. I was definitely in this space like okay, you know, can I do this? I've always been a person who believed in execution. I'd always been the person my friends could depend on and call on for anything. But could I start a business? From scratch?

Even though I had been "that person" in general, for me it really became about, what the next part of my life would look like. I had always been a pretty good student, an even better networker and student of people. And I'd always had plans for a better life, but many of those plans were aligned with wanting to create a better life for my mother, the life I felt she deserved.

When my mother passed away, I felt like that was taken from me. I wanted to give her the opportunity to really live, as she had worked so hard so much of her life as a single mother, as a loving sister and daughter, and I wanted her to be able to reap the rewards of what she had invested in me. With that opportunity gone, I had to really think about what I was doing all of this for. You'll have to ask yourself at some point the same question: What are you doing all of this for?

Not too soon after that, I felt I had refound my "why." I wanted to build a company to help other people solve their problems. I wanted to build a legacy. I wanted to create opportunities via economic mobility offered to people in the form of a well-paying career that they loved and a company they could grow in.

I wanted my community to understand that just when they thought they couldn't make it another year, another day that things could still work out for them—that they could still lead a life they had imagined and a life they could be the architect of. I was also talking to myself, and I'm also saying this to you.

I wanted to help people, and not just those who were in my household. I wanted to go beyond that, and have a bigger impact on people's lives.

I wanted to create generational wealth.

That was the impact that my parents' deaths had on me.

Yet, I know that losing someone close to you, whether that is in death or through some other form of separation, can be devastating. It can have a different effect, and many find it hard to recover. For me, my parents dying at a young age in my life made me work harder.

Also, in my subconscious, I realized I didn't really have anyone to turn to. I didn't have the normal home to retreat to, especially when you hear these stories of successful founders working out of their parents, basements or homes to get their businesses off the ground.

When I think about founders from communities of color and otherwise, supporting our families rises to the top of our reasons of why we do what we do.

I never was able to realize buying my mother the home of her dreams, or retiring her so she didn't have to work until she couldn't physically do so anymore. Now I'd pour my days and time into building—building a company that seeks to enrich communities so that those with less have more.

Because of this new vision, my first company was heavily geared toward helping community figures, nonprofits, and those aligned with social good, to get their programs and ideas off the ground. We wanted to ensure that they were effectively operating and able to serve the communities that needed them the most.

It took some time, but you have to think of yourself as an entrepreneur, a business owner, a builder; otherwise you'll spend a lot of time downplaying what you do and what you are seeking to accomplish. Yes, you could fail and the odds are you'll fail at a lot of things along the way, perhaps even that thing you created and wanted most. I know I did and still do. Yet, I've learned my strengths and my weaknesses and seek out the strengths in others to create balance. I don't desire to be a jack of all trades. I desire to do what I do, best.

A lot of times we are waiting for the perfect moment or the perfect feeling. Lisa Nichols, an author and motivational speaker who often talks about overcoming doubt and fear, said it best: "do it afraid." You really have to sit in that for a second, because you can wait for years or never get started at all waiting to feel something different. Something that doesn't feel like anxiety or fear or doesn't give off nervous energy.

I am often asked if I get nervous. Sometimes I can speak on a large stage and feel no anxiety, and other times I can speak in front of a group of teenagers and feel the pressure of wanting to leave an impression that could potentially alter their future, the way that some speakers have done for me.

Either way, you have to find what motivates you—what's going to push you after a long day when you don't want to go anymore, or you are feeling the weight of success or failure.

I talk about my upbringing because it's important for people to understand my journey, especially those who come from a similar background as I do. I want everyone to know that if I did it with so few resources, then you can do it too, and most likely even better.

People often ask me what my favorite part is about the work that I do. For me, it's about building a company that is mission-driven, one that I feel, as my mentor told me, I can make money and do good too with. But most importantly, I want the people who work with me to feel empowered to utilize their own capabilities and their own skill sets.

I want them, as well as digging deep to make great products, to sell great products, and to be a part of a team that markets great products, to know that they're part of something that's really helping the world and helping the community we are fostering do their work better.

I want them to make a lasting impact and really create something that is beyond what they had imagined. Building SGI and now Resilia is something that I feel really embodies our mission of powering the people changing the world.

When I think about my favorite part of the work that I do, it would be building a company and employing people to be able to do this work. It's not about necessarily building this huge hundred-million-dollar annual recurring revenue company, it's about whether we can build products that move the needle and raise the bar.

You'll have to remind yourself often of the reason that got you started.

I often have to remind myself of why I started because I think that's important, too. As much as they try to tell you otherwise, business is personal. I think about how I spend my time, where my mind goes to, and where my thoughts lead me to so I can recenter when I need to, reinforcing what really matters.

As an entrepreneur you have to keep positivity in your life. If you wake up in the morning and you're like, oh, you know, this is going to be a dreadful day, or if it's Wednesday, and you're telling yourself it's the middle of the week and I just have to keep pushing to Friday until it's over, that mindset takes over your entire aura and embodies who you become.

Instead, you want to wake up and realize you have another day to get it right. Another day to get what is in front of you done. If you need to rest for a day or a week, then do it. What matters is that you're doing things that align with your whole self, right? You're doing things that make you feel good and you have to reaffirm yourself. That's so important because not everyone will. I had to learn over time how to live in a healthy state of mind. I'm a sponge when it comes to learning. I want to learn as much as possible, and in business you are constantly learning, but what are you absorbing? I listen to what people are dishing out and I soak up what I need and I release the rest. I have to, because we're in the age of over information.

Yet, in order for me to become a really good entrepreneur and business owner, I had to learn what I didn't know. When I first started out, I began to reach out to people who were in business who had ascended to greater heights, to where I wanted to go.

I think it's important to seek people out because they have insights that they're able to recall from their journey in a way that was exciting for me to listen to. It was exciting to understand what mistakes they had made so I could try to avoid some of them, although I'd make enough of my own. But I listened because the more you learn the more you can minimize the mistakes, and when you're building a business that's critical.

At the end of the day you have these people in your life as business mentors, or guides as I often call them, and you're trying to figure out how to win, how to play this game, how to be better than the next, and if you're in tech, probably faster than the next, too.

I grew up in a single-parent household. My mother raised four of us on a salary of $29,000 a year. She was an assistant manager at Kmart, running their gardening department. My mother worked hard for whomever she was working for and everything she did, she did with excellence. She passed that down to my siblings and me.

My mother was my role model, although she herself had not graduated from college. My grandmother had not received a formal education past the sixth grade but would live to be 103 years old. She was also my role model.

Do you know where your story begins? My entrepreneurship story began where my mother's story left off.

When I started SGI and then when I entered tech I was ready to work hard, but I knew I was behind. I knew that there was a knowledge curve that I had to really overcome. I wasn't out in Silicon Valley. I wasn't in New York. I wasn't in a hotbed for tech, and so I had to get really resourceful.

2 The Difference

The biggest risk of all is not taking one.
—Mellody Hobson

My good friend Sherrell Dorsey, founder of TP Insights, referred to me as the "antithesis" in an article she published for her editorial and tech platform, *The Plug*.

I'm female, Black, from the South, and a nontechnical solo founder. In all respects (and perhaps statistics), I'm everything that they say a tech founder can't be.

Overall, I've now been an entrepreneur for over 12 years, and what a roller-coaster ride it has been, from bootstrapping my first company Solid Ground Innovations (SGI) to raising capital for my second company. It's been more than what I could have imagined, and really little of what I expected. But what could I have expected, being that I had no true blueprint starting out?

Yet, I feel that entrepreneurship was in my veins. Do you remember starting or selling anything, from Girl Scout cookies to lemonade stands? I never did either, but I did sell candy for my school's annual fundraiser. Looking back, that was a form of entrepreneurship mixed with hustle, too.

In this book, a lot of lessons are transferable to mostly all entrepreneurs regardless of sector, though I'll spend most of my time focused on walking you through the steps of launching and raising capital for Resilia, the tech company I launched in 2016. If you want a more detailed description of how I built Solid Ground Innovations, the professional services company

I started in 2009, I have an entire self-published book on that. called Solid Ground. But let's start from the top of my entrepreneurship journey. When I was 19 years old, I rallied up my friends to help me start an online newspaper that I would name *B-NOW* (*Black News Our Way*). I remember talking to my college professor, Dr. Leonard Moore, about the idea. I told him that I wanted to bring together students from Southern University A&M College, a neighboring HBCU (historically Black college or university), and students from Louisiana State University A&M, a predominantly white institution, where I attended school. He was all onboard and asked me if I had filed an LLC. He might as well have been speaking a foreign language, because I had no worldly idea of what he was talking about other than it was something I perhaps needed to run a business. There in his office he wrote me a check for $150. Looking back, I guess I could say he was my very first investor. He was at least the very first person who believed in me and gave me money for an idea. He also understood that there would be costs associated with my idea.

It wasn't until a year or two ago that I acknowledged *B-NOW* as what in hindsight was my first business. My first hires were also students at LSU. Terry and Jonathan created my website. Another friend created my logo. I suspect it cost a few hundred bucks at the time: $50 for a logo, maybe $200 for the website with all pages included. I even enlisted my friends to write articles and to act as administrators, and hired my friend Scott to take our photos in the recreational room of the west campus apartments. I had an all-hands meeting on campus as well in Coates Hall, where I enlisted other friends to write stories for *B-NOW*.

Maybe I didn't know it then, but I had created something special. A few years later, at 22 years old, I would start Solid Ground Innovations.

But I was now in grad school. My mother had passed away. I was consulting while I worked at an organization called Louisiana CASA (Court Appointed Special Advocates) as an AmeriCorps VISTA member while going to grad school full-time. I know technically you weren't supposed to go to school during your AmeriCorps service, but it actually came very naturally to me.

At Louisiana CASA, I worked mostly on their advocacy programs and state capital projects. During this time an opportunity came about for me to start consulting for a new foundation, so I took it. This would eventually turn into an opportunity that led my work to receiving a Nobel Prize for public service, the Jefferson Award, and being recognized in the White House Report to the Senate on Volunteerism in America as the director of TTI, a nonprofit started by Tyrus Thomas, mostly running the organization, and an award-winning youth program we had created called C.A.T.C.H. (Caring and Actively Teaching Children Hope).

It was during these early days that I really learned how to operate an organization. So when I launched my first business to the public it felt right, even if I didn't feel 100% ready—though doing the actual work would prove we never ever really feel 100% ready. We just do it. We take the leap.

So, in 2009 I started SGI; we were a strategic communications and management agency with an arm called SGI Cares, which helped nonprofit organizations and grant makers such as the W.K. Kellogg Foundation provide capacity support via technical assistance to the organizations that they fund.

For nonprofits, we were acting as their back office in lieu of full-time employees. In my clients, I'd meet some of my biggest champions like Raymond Jetson the President and CEO of Metromorphosis, a nonprofit with a mission to transform urban communities from within.

When I first started SGI I didn't have employees. We were a true professional services agency and because of this we were able to stay very lean as a business. I began creating marketing materials (trust me, nothing fancy at all). One underutilized resource I leaned on was using our local state economic development office. There I was able to use state-funded programs to cover the cost of items I needed to start my business, such as marketing and collateral materials. I participated in programs that can be found within every state. In Louisiana it was called Economic Gardening. I'm pretty certain that at the time we went through this program, we were not as large as the other businesses. But we were able to take advantage of consultants to discuss opportunities related to sales, operations, and understanding our competitive landscape. Having experienced individuals to even just talk through my ideas with and get feedback from was a game changer. I always urge small businesses to take advantage of their local, state, and federal programs and the free resources they provide; if nothing else, at least find out what exists.

There are many ways to build a business. When I started SGI, there was so much I didn't know. I was so green, from state filing docs to understanding the operational and legal jargon to writing winning proposals that would ultimately land me my first clients.

There is truth to the saying "you don't know what you don't know." This is the case for all of us when it comes to a subject matter that is unfamiliar to us. SGI was a strategic communications and management agency. Early on we heavily specialized in nonprofit management, hence where the idea for Resilia came from.

Some of the projects we took on then, I'd never touch today. I'm just being honest.

I know there is a lot of talk about getting your value and what you are worth. But when you are just starting out, and you are trying to get clients and prove yourself, as well as figure out your pricing, it's very possible there will be times you undercut yourself. Sometimes it will be worth it and other times not so much.

As I began to establish my credibility and footing, everything around me began to increase, including my rates.

One thing in business you'll have to look out for is "upside-down contracts." This is where your cost to do the work exceeds the price you are charging, and thus your business loses money in the execution of the work. These types of agreements are easier to recover from when it's just you working on a project, but when you layer employees or other hired consultants on top it can be difficult to recover from.

A few years into my business, I started resigning from contracts because of this. Not because the clients were horrible, but because they didn't make economic sense. One of my close advisors told me a long time ago that you get into business to make a profit. This may be your first reason, or it may be one of many reasons after the initial passion and your purpose drives you to start it. Either way, it's a business for a reason.

As SGI started to grow, we started to reevaluate SGI Cares, the arm that focused solely on nonprofits. SGI was growing—a very uncomfortable growth, but growing nevertheless. A few years in, we had landed our first seven-figure, multi-year contract with a healthcare provider seeking to provide Medicaid services via a government contract. They found us through a state website that listed Hudson initiative–approved companies. The program encourages state agencies to contract with certified small businesses, as well as encouraging contractors who receive contracts from the state to use good-faith efforts to utilize certified small businesses in the performance of the contract. If that contract taught us anything, it was the importance of cash flow and billing. When you are dealing with government contracts and large agencies, the billing cycles are much longer. Yet, because of the size of the contract, you have to hire employees and/or contractors to do the work. We also had to execute media buying and other vendor purchases as an agreement of the contract. It's very important to have someone, if not yourself, who knows the intricacies of buying media and appropriately running a tight ship with budgeting and billing. Otherwise, this can cause various headaches, from delayed payments from the client to your business struggling to meet important deadlines such as payroll because you're awaiting payment.

So, as SGI continued to grow I decided that we needed to go in a different direction with our SGI Cares arm. Via this arm, we were serving nonprofits in various ways. But not all nonprofits are created (or treated) equal, and many struggle to find additional room in their budgets to hire consultants. When they do, consultants can find themselves wanting to go above and beyond to help the nonprofit organization, because they can really get drawn into the work. As SGI began to grow we no longer had the capacity to service nonprofits in the way we had become accustomed to; when you're acting as a back office it's very natural that circumstances change and that the workload changes as well. So, I started thinking about ways we could continue to support these entities.

I really began to think about the future of our space as I saw it: software as a service.

We were providing a service and we began to think about how we could productize that service and deliver it through a software solution. We are seeing technology being evolved for various sectors by the experts in those sectors, thus what a technology founder once looked like is changing. Experts in their particular area of expertise are thinking about how they can create technology solutions for their antiquated sector in order to evolve it through the use of technology, and simplify a lot of the problems that they're having through solution-based products.

So, I began to think about how I could do this in the nonprofit and philanthropy sector, and ultimately how this technology could extend into other verticals such as government.

Yet, the first service that we took a stab at productizing was one that we offered under SGI Cares, called nonprofit creation services. We were helping nonprofits go through tedious paperwork to file for incorporation and exemption for their nonprofit, which today we call formation services.

We had created a system, and were receiving referrals from attorneys and accountants and other clients to provide this service. We were working with schools. We were working with health clinics. Many of them came to us because they wanted to create a nonprofit arm; the same for small businesses, restaurants—you name it.

And so we felt that there was perhaps an opportunity to create technology around this service, as we were doing it manually, which was very time-consuming. Then people were coming to us because they had tried their luck with products like Legal-Zoom which was heavily focused on just prepping the services, and customers still had no idea what to do next.

So as we continued to think about how we could release the manual touches that we were having with this service, pro-ductization seemed like the most likely solution. In November 2016, we launched what was then called Exempt Me Now to the public. We were doing something really simple and that was productizing or "TurboTaxing," as we would say, the pro-cess of incorporation and exemption nonprofits. We launched the product in all 50 states, allowing our customers to now go online and "do it yourself, but not by yourself."

I talk a bit about how we assembled the team to get this product launched later.

We were ultimately trying to solve for the bottleneck of com-munication that existed via emails and calls, standardizing the process, improving approval timelines, thus drastically reducing the time it took an average customer to go through the complete process from prep to filing to securing their exemption.

We wanted to go beyond just being a prep service, instead taking those customers from A through Z from prep to filing, and educating them throughout the process, so they understood what would be next as founders of nonprofits. Now that product was in market those customers began asking for other services. They were asking, What happens next? How do I run effective board meetings? How do I raise money?

How do I create brand and awareness for my cause in my community? And so we continued to think about how we could further productize the services that we were offering as consultants and continue to deliver these services through a software solution. And so the next product that we were thinking about was the nonprofit platform (NPX). The NPX platform was a natural second product because we could now begin delivering the capacity support that we were offering as consultants through a subscription-based platform, whether that was fundraising, curriculum design, or providing resources such as conflict interest statements to development materials, and finance tools to help manage budgets and funding, and how to stay on track and align to reporting milestones that are required for certain grants.

Yet, there was still something missing. As consultants, we knew that there were major silos that existed between organizations and the funders that granted to them. Additionally, there was usually a number of us hired to do various projects related to one program whether that was evaluation, technical assistance, or some other task.

The enterprise platform would be the next product we would launch in the market. This product would compliment the NPX platform to allow funders to provide the capacity support and technical assistance that we were providing to organizations on a touch-and-go basis year-round. Additionally, funders would have access to their own dashboard, which would allow them to capture insights and evaluations, report information in real time regarding their projects, and easily manage stakeholders such as board members. So, whether you were a public charity, foundation, government entity, or corporation, you could benefit from this product. This one-app solution would be geared toward solving a few hurdles: scaling impact, measuring impact over time, and allowing grant recipients to deliver reports directly to their funders without the heavy load of reporting and in the manner funders want to see it.

I was asked by Keely Anson, an investor at Incite Partners, why I wanted to democratize philanthropy. She admitted that her question was almost rhetorical in a sense because she knew why. Incite, though a venture fund, also had a nonprofit that supported organizations that aligned to their company mission of launching and backing the most important and innovative ideas in the country. Sometimes this doesn't look like a startup. Sometimes these ideas are within nonprofits. Because of this, Keely had worked with several of Incite's nonprofit partners and regardless of size she found the same challenges to be prevalent.

So, we began to build out our enterprise product to do a number of things but certainly to create a more harmonious flow between funders and their grant recipients.

Exempt Me Now would go through a rebrand to recognize our suite of products, and what would come out of that is Resilia, a SaaS technology platform that enables organizations to increase capacity, and enterprises (think cities, private foundations, and corporations) to scale impact.

I share this part of my journey to emphasize that you have to start somewhere. As you'll recall me mentioning, I'm not a technical founder, but if you have an idea and you're willing to execute against it, anything is possible. Today entrepreneurship has been glamorized in so many ways. I'm here to tell you that it's hard, and that success is achievable, but there's very little glamour in it at all. I'm excited to see all the aspiring entrepreneurs, and those who have broken through to attain success.

As a Black female entrepreneur, I'm among the fastest-growing demographic of new business owners. What we often don't talk much about is that the average Black female–led business generates less than $30,000 a year. Digitalundivided, a nonprofit studied the effects of the COVID-19 pandemic on Black female founders, finding that 82% reported a loss of revenue because of the crisis.

I do not say that we should start businesses to make money because I believe money is everything. But security is something, the security to take care of your family and/or yourself. What I know for sure is that not having financial security will make your days much longer, and will likely cause you an unhealthy amount of stress, but it's something that business owners often face on their climb. Coupling that with running a business and one that doesn't provide you the financial security you need in order to pay your bills will make it difficult to focus on growing your business because you're too focused on just trying to keep your head afloat and survive, literally.

The life of an entrepreneur can feel like you are on a roller coaster: there are a lot of ups and downs, you can't always see what turns are ahead of you, and the roller coaster can seem never ending. At one point you'll be having a high, perhaps a new product launch or amazing press that captures the essence of what you are doing and building; at another point there can be what feels like endless things going wrong. Customers complain, key team members move on, or you just feel burned out. Something that my mother shared with me that I now apply to entrepreneurship, not just my personal life, is: "Don't let your lows get so low you can't see the heavens, or your highs so high you can't touch the ground."

2020 was a year of extreme highs and lows for me: just days before closing on my Series A round, COVID-19 began to rear its ugly little head, and I could feel my anxiety doing the same. I remember emailing my attorney, "We need to get our round closed!" I could feel the ground shifting—and just like that, it did.

Later, I'll get to how I raised a Series A during the onset of COVID-19, but first, let's take a step back and discuss what's needed for this journey.

Focus

Whether you are starting a bootstrapped business or what you hope to be a venture-backable startup, it's important to focus and really hone in on what it is you want to achieve.

Entrepreneurs or aspiring entrepreneurs often reach out to me to ask how to get started, and one of the biggest challenges

I find they have is the inability to focus long enough to get started and then the inability to retain that focus to create consistent momentum. If you are someone who generally hops from one idea to the next, it could be because you lack focus. It also may be connected to what I describe as a "hustle mentality." I'm not speaking of a hustle mentality that comes from a desire to get things done no matter what, but instead a mentality that finds you jumping from what seems like one opportunity to the next without truly having an end goal in mind. Though you might have success here, what I've found is that this mentality can leave you short-sighted, and success will often feel fleeting.

When starting something new, it's important to get focused and spend some time fleshing out your ideas, figuring out whether this is something you're truly passionate about. Will you keep going if you don't have any funding? Will you even start? Are you willing to make the necessary sacrifices that come along with everything that's about to happen to you? Are you willing to constantly have to level up and push yourself?

Have you figured out what your goals are and how to get really focused on how to build momentum? How do you put together the right ingredients to actually begin to grow not just your idea but yourself?

I know it's hard. It's hard for me. If you are a builder and an entrepreneur you probably have no shortage of ideas. And you know, that's something that motivates you. Right?

I think particularly that there is this theme that's being cemented in us. We're focused on how we create multiple streams of revenue, but when you think about individuals like Warren Buffett and how most people created their wealth, it's because they focus on that thing that really took off for them and became really good at that. That's the thing people reached out to them for.

You start by nailing that first idea, cultivating it, building it, and executing it, and then from there you diversify. So when you think about that you really want to focus on figuring that one thing out. You don't want to be a jack of all trades but a master of none.

So, what is your niche? What are you really good at? It doesn't mean your niche has to be a small market but it's one that you can distinguish yourself in as the thought leader in your space and you can work toward building that one thing first.

If you have too much on your plate, you will constantly feel disheveled.

So now you have this disheveled mind where you have all these thoughts and ideas running through your brain and you have an endless list of tasks that you're trying to get through and you begin to do those tasks in a mediocre way. So think about how you can tune out the things that are making you inefficient.

Why am I talking about focus so much in this chapter? Because the rest of this book is honing in on how to build your business or startup idea; how to raise capital and close deals without being backed by investors. But none of it will be useful if your intent is to move the needle in your business if you aren't focused and don't understand what is required of you for this next level of your life.

How do you cut out the noise? Some things I do to realign are:

1. Meditation
2. Saying no
3. Time blocking
4. Mentorship

One reason I wrote this book is because small changes in your daily habits can really have a huge impact on how you take on the day, and how you take on the day will impact how successful you are. Another reason I wrote this book is because I know that not everyone has mentors and I strongly believe that information should be easy to access for all.

3 Bootstrapping versus Raising Capital

You don't have to have every single step figured out before you venture out and do something.

—Lisa Price

As cliché as it may sound, most great things *really don't* happen overnight.

Professional Services to Startup

So, it's 2016, and I have an idea for what would soon become Resilia. At the time, my marketing director knew of my aspirations to turn my nonprofit startup services into a software solution. We flew out to San Francisco and met a guy by the name of Ismail. Ismail was so influential in the early success of the technical side of my product that I would end up giving him shares later down the road (when they were actually worth something).

Nonetheless, here I was in San Francisco, embarking on what would become my first venture-backed startup journey.

Now, don't confuse "startup" with "business." They have some crossover similarities, but startups face challenges unique to the space that "businesses" do not. For instance, pictures of Mark Zuckerberg or Elon Musk don't represent businesses as much as they do startups. For a new business (not necessarily a startup), there is usually a product demand or product/market fit. Many times, there may be no innovation or inventiveness at all, rather just supplying an existing market demand—but for startups, not so much. For reference and throughout this book, I'll refer to Solid Ground Innovations (or SGI) as a small business and Resilia as a startup so that you know the difference.

There was a conversation on Twitter about which was harder. I receive that question often. Which is harder—building a business that is bootstrapped or building a venture-backed startup? The key thing to know is that most startups don't start off as funded. The journey to being a venture-backed company comes with its own set of obstacles. When you think about the reasons why funded startups fail and why bootstrapped startups fail they're very similar. Funded startups fail because the business model isn't viable, it doesn't have enough traction, it lacks financing and investors, it has technical and product issues, there is no market need, it's bad timing, there is a lack of focus, or it has pricing or cost issues. Why do bootstrapped businesses fail? One reason is that the business model is not viable, though I'd argue that it depends on the business, as bootstrapped businesses tend to lean toward products and services with less friction to enter the market. I'd go as far as to say that businesses often fail because of their inability to close customers, whereas startups tend to be more disruptive: there's no market need, they lacked financing, they lacked focus, or, of course, they ran out of cash. I'd add that bootstrapped companies fail because they grow too fast without a sustainable cash source to keep the business afloat. Sound familiar to startups? It should.

Why Businesses Fail	
Bootstrapped	**Venture-Backed**
Ran out of cash	Technical/product issues
Pricing issues	No market need
Business model not sustainable	Not enough traction
Lacked financing	No market need
Clash with partners	Clash with co-founders
Lack of focus	Lacked financing/investors
Can't find customers (no market need)	Lack of focus
Can't retain or attract new customers	Business model not viable
Ran out of cash	Ran out of cash

Yet, startups are glorified in a way that small businesses tend to not be, especially if that startup has raised capital. I would know. We are looking at social media and the headlines through the lens of instant gratification when, generally speaking, most founders are putting in years and years and years of hard work, generally having a lot of ups and downs along the way.

Do I prefer bootstrapping over raising capital? Before I had ever raised a dollar for my startup, I bootstrapped a company to seven figures without any capital, and highly likely had I not pivoted into technology it would have grown much larger. Yet, I don't think there was this moment where I made a decision to bootstrap my company. It was more so the cards I had been dealt with. At the time, I knew I would have to build my company brick by brick as there were no financial resources available to me then. I knew I would have to be scrappy and win business in order to grow, so I did just that. Now that I have a bootstrapped company under my belt that was very successful (and have raised venture for a second company) there is one thing I can say that I know is true—bootstrapping gives you freedom and flexibility in a way that raising capital or outside financing doesn't.

On the Bootstrapping Process

SGI is a true bootstrapped business. I built it by overseeing services that I could accomplish as a sole owner. Once I had built enough clients I started hiring one team member at a time at first. My first hire was more of a generalist, but that was sound when it came to logistics because, let's be honest, when you are bootstrapping, your first hire should be someone who gets stuff done! The way we went about securing contracts is actually subcontracting under larger companies. If there is one word of advice I can give it's that you have to learn fast, and there's no better way to learn your field than by working (still as a business owner) with someone who has done what you are seeking to do at scale.

I faced no shortage of challenges closing contracts, as a woman, a Black woman, a young person (which to some can come off as inexperience), or as a person from the South. I would recommend bootstrapping for as long as you can. As someone who has bootstrapped their first company and now raised over $10 million for a second one, I can't stress enough that you have to calculate what you want to give up and ensure it's a price you are willing to pay. It may have taken me longer with bootstrapping but it also allowed me to invest the first money into my second company, which has allowed me to retain more ownership as I was able to use cash as an incentive and not equity earlier on.

Remember, bootstrapping is when you are building a company with just your savings or, in my case, the income I was making from our first client sales.

So, is it easier to bootstrap a business? Some would say yes, I'd argue no. Yet, I do believe there are key factors you should take into account when trying to understand the economics behind what it will take to bootstrap a company without other financial resources (a rich uncle, investors, a loan, etc.). Some things to consider are: Is it inexpensive to start? Do you need inventory or hardware? Is it something you can do on your own, meaning, do you have to hire people out of the gate? Is there an audience you can sell to?

For me, my first company was a consultancy agency and, although I didn't know it at the time, it answered all of those questions. I was able to take the money from sales and reinvest to help me grow the business, without investors or outside capital. Once the business was more successful and we started bringing on larger clients, I was able to draw down on a line of credit to make sure we could manage vendor payments and other necessities while we waited for payment from clients. When thinking about bootstrapping, understand that it's predicated on your ability to efficiently run the business on its own revenue. This means that you have to be really good with money management and making the right decisions that don't have a negative cash flow impact on the business. When starting your own business, especially if you are a first-time owner, this can be very difficult. I for one have made my fair share of costly mistakes that, if I hadn't been able to recover quickly, could have taken the company under. When you are just starting off you're going to look around at your competitive landscape and think that the only way to compete is that you'll need all the resources the winners in your space need. Yet, budgeting for absolute needs is going to be critical. You have to make the most viable decision for your business and separate "needs" from "wants."

One of the biggest hurdles for businesses that are bootstrapping can be managing a budget and cash flow into the business. We were heavily involved in government contracting and anyone who has ever worked with the government knows they either pay you really quickly or really slowly. Additionally, even with our private contracts we had to bill after the work was completed. We had to float hundreds of thousands of dollars at times in media buys; this is where relationships with vendors will become important. With proper vendor agreements you will be able to do business with certain vendors and pay them when you get paid, allowing you to keep cash on hand. Yet, for smaller vendors, if you want to show good business acumen you'll need to pay some times ahead of receiving payment, which can be hard.

There are obviously advantages and disadvantages with bootstrapping. It's not for every type of business model. For Resilia, it would have been almost impossible to bootstrap the idea, at least to scale. But there are some upsides to bootstrapping, the biggest advantage being the control you retain over your business. You have control over where you reinvest profits, and you are in control financially because it's essentially your money.

There are, however, some disadvantages. Many will ask what made me start a new business when my first one was doing well. For me SGI was always going to be a great business, but I wanted and felt I had the ability to really scale something to greater heights with the use of technology. One of the disadvantages of bootstrapping is that your business grows slower. If you only have minimal cash, your business can only grow so quickly. You also take on a larger personal financial risk when bootstrapping a company. I started Resilia by bootstrapping and you can imagine the anxiety as over time I pumped more and more cash into the business prior to raising, a million dollars to be exact. I was sure that it was worth it and was betting on myself in a big way, so I was willing to make the investment, but pumping that type of money—my own money—into a company for someone like me, a first-generation college student, was scary. What if it failed? What if I never recouped what I personally invested? Had I made the wrong choice?

When thinking of bootstrapping a startup you really have to be in it for the service or the product you are providing because it may take some time before you see any profit, if you ever see any at all. The other thing to be mindful of is that if you are in a space where competitive advantage or capturing market share is important, you will certainly be at a disadvantage. this usually is the case for startups.

If you are bootstrapping a business and finances are a concern then you have to pick the right type of business one that generates cash fairly quickly, needs less early capital to get going, might allow you to barter services, might allow you to leverage partners, and one that might allow you to work from home or a coffee shop.

As your bootstrapped company starts to grow, things can start to get a little rocky. You need to hire people; you might need to make an investment to launch a new product or to fulfill a new project. That's all grand, but don't lose sight of the fact that money is the lifeline to your business. Cash is still king.

So when you don't actually have investors or investment capital being infused into your company to grow it, the alternative is to grow it by landing and expanding customers and accounts.

Those of you who are just starting out may be wondering how to land your first customer or how to land the next customer or how to land the key account that's a game changer. For me, the account that literally changed the landscape for SGI was an account that I landed with Aetna Better Health.

They were working with the state and the Department of Health to be one of the providers for the state's Medicaid program, and the individual who was overseeing that transition was based in Connecticut.

She was searching for companies by utilizing the small business Hudson Initiative website and found my first company, Solid Ground Innovations, through the Opportunity Louisiana.com website.

The website listed all the different incentives for businesses that have certifications and our business at the time was located in an area that was covered under the Hudson Initiative program.

So that location put me in an area of Baton Rouge, Louisiana, that was deemed an opportunity for growth. Today there are several programs, such as HUD or Opportunity Zones, that incentivize businesses that are located within certain zip codes. Even at Resilia we had a fund that wanted to invest in our company but we had to be located in an Opportunity Zone. So, if it applies, make sure you are taking advantage of these programs, as they have been beneficial for both SGI and Resilia.

We were an approved vendor and the lead at Aetna Better Health was sourcing different companies to reach out to, and she found us on the website and reached out to schedule a call. She was working out of their Phoenix office, and knew nothing about Louisiana other than that she was tasked with this massive goal to open up an office there that would grow to hundreds of people within a year.

She saw what we were doing. She saw that we were essentially embedded in the community and she wanted to speak to me. She wanted to see whether we could fulfill the project and the work. That was a memorable moment because it was a seven-figure multi-year contract; we stood to make a pretty substantial amount of money from it, and it would prove to be transformative for the company, allowing us to grow faster and take on larger contracts by strengthening our portfolio. Another advantage is that it also allowed me to increase our capabilities and strengthen our knowledge base to execute for the world's largest companies.

Think about how you are positioning yourself as a company not only for the opportunities you are seeking, but also for making yourself visible for the opportunities that people and agencies are seeking. These are some of the things business owners should be thinking about as well: you're always looking for opportunities, but how are you preparing your company and yourself for when an opportunity does come to you? Can you execute it? Can you build up the capacity through a string of contractors or hire full-time employees if need be, to execute the work because you have built that rapport with others? You have to be ready for when the opportunity knocks because if you do the work, it will.

With Aetna, we were able to put together a proposal that broke down the population, partnerships opportunities, and how we would approach advertising and marketing for them as well as help them build and deepen relationships with key stakeholders. It was compelling.

We had never worked in the healthcare sector before, but we learned quickly and devised a plan to execute the work that was in front of us while preparing on the backend to retain the contract and build whatever capacity would be needed for the long haul. We had the community contacts and the political contacts to create partnerships that were real and authentic; in areas we lacked in, we made up for it tenfold there. We got the contract.

We got the contract over agencies that were far bigger than ours that had way more capacity than ours. Then from there we had to build up the capacity to actually service that customer. This is where I was definitely tested as a business owner because early on we did have to float some of those contracts from having to buy media. And because we had never bought media of that size, we didn't have vendor credit yet. We hadn't built the credit to be able to buy media and then pay back our vendors once we got paid, and so we had to pay upfront a lot of that money. We had to draw down on a line of credit to help us get through, but it taught me a lot about managing cash flow and setting expectations with your subcontractors.

Though this contract was the largest at the time, we had dozens and dozens of other contracts as well that we had to ensure were being properly serviced. So, I was executing work, trying to meet payroll, moving all of these balls with two hands at the same time, but I was getting it done—just not without some failure along the way.

This contract would open up other opportunities to government contracting.

What enticed me to go deeper in government contracting was when I heard Necole Parker, the CEO and founder of The Elocen Group from Atlanta, who was leading a workshop and discussing how she got into government contracting at a Black Enterprise Entrepreneurs Summit conference. She described her early experience in government contracting as a "feast or famine" kind of existence, as she would land small contracts but they would end soon, and then she would be chasing the next one.

She spoke about being a single mother and how in order to start her first business she had decided to move in with her mother to save money. She had actually started off working for another company doing program management, a minority-owned business group that only did federal contracting. She had been denied a promotion, though she was responsible for over 70% of the contracts the company brought in. She talked about how she walked away depressed and crying. After that, she set off on her own. Parker has now grown The Elocen Group into a multimillion-dollar program and project management business. She credits much of her success to having become an 8(a) certified business.

What really drew me in about Necole's story is that she also started bootstrapped. Having moved back in with her parents to save money and start a business, she began to land very small contracts over time. Then she won a $1 million subcontract with a larger company, also known in the federal contracting space as a Prime. After that, she landed one of her largest contracts to date, a $50 million, five-year contract with the Food and Drug Administration.

Understanding what it takes to win doesn't come automatically, but with hard work, resilience, and the willingness to learn what you don't know, it does come.

A decade of sweat, tears, and hard work will make you look like an overnight success story.

Repeatable and Predictable Revenue, Regardless

For me, regardless of whether I were bootstrapping or not, I wanted repeatable, predictable methods of attaining opportunities, wins, and, most importantly, revenue. But, as with everything you desire most, it takes time to create a playbook that works for your operation.

Social media has changed the world as we know it. It has also changed the business landscape and made it easier to get started and become a business owner than ever before. But I always have to remind people that we are also watching people's highlight reels for what took many years to build. Yes, there are some cases of people getting there faster than most, but in reality it takes 10 years (or more, in some instances) to get to a level of success where you might now feel like you can breathe. I'm now 12 years in business and it's still a marathon for me. I'm just now reaping some of the rewards from successes I've had.

What has worked for me and what I've also tried to adopt and create within business is creating repeatable processes.

If you are in SaaS then you've probably heard the words repeatable and predictable a thousand times, but this is no coincidence. When something works and when it is tried and true, you stick with it.

Whether those things are big or small, within your business or even within your personal life, they're important because they create a level of consistency that's needed to be successful. It also creates a level of dependability in which you can depend on something most likely happening as a result of your work. Then you just drive that.

So, how can you hone in on what you're really good at and then repeat that over and over and over and over for your customers? For yourself?

That's what drew me to SaaS products. The ability to create repeatable and scalable products that you can sell over and over.

Money Can't Be the Only Motivation

I know I've talked a good bit already about revenue and the importance of making money. We often push starting a business off of passion, but let's be clear, money can be a motivation. I actually feel that it's a privilege when people say the opposite. If you were just fired from your job and don't have savings to fall back on, and you have to pay your bills and take care of your family, then yes, money will likely be the motivation. But when you are bootstrapping a business you have to think about what really motivates you to keep going and to keep reinvesting your own money, resources, and time into it. Because of the investment that it often takes to jumpstart a business, you are thinking far beyond money; it's what wakes you up in the middle of the night that forces you to write down that idea before you go back to sleep.

People say that business isn't personal but how can it not be, when you've invested this much time and energy into it? When entrepreneurs have taken out second mortgages on their homes, and maxed out their credit cards for it? When you've built it from nothing, business certainly does become personal, because it is a testament to what you have created and what you've gone through to do it.

When your livelihood depends on your success, is that not personal? So what motivates you to keep running a business? What gets you up in the morning? What do you think about late at night when it's just you?

For me it's a number of things. How do I help my team get better and ensure that they have the resources they need to be successful?

I've already talked about how the death of my mother was my motivator to start a business.

But even more so, entrepreneurship was my gateway to being a builder. I am truly a builder. Once I identify what it is that is standing in my way I begin to think about paths I can take to eliminate any barriers that I might encounter that stand in my way.

For example, people often ask me how they can build a great network, as having a great network can't be understated.

Your network will open up opportunities for you. It's how you get referrals. It's how you close a deal that seemed out of reach. For a bootstrapped company, it's how you get that growth in Q3 that you weren't anticipating. Building a strong network can help you grow your business.

I've already mentioned the importance of choosing the right business if you are going to bootstrap. SGI was the right business because we were an agency. There were no high overhead costs to start. We essentially started it with sweat equity.

When bootstrapping with your own resources you have to find the lowest entry point with the fewest barriers for you to enter and start your business as a whole. Not having funds is not a reason to not get started; you can't let that deter you from your entrepreneurial dreams.

Without an infusion of capital you are going to have to cover your basic expenses, depending on your business. Some people are utilizing the money that they are making from their day job to fuel their dreams.

This also doesn't mean you are short-changing your current employer. Let's go back to the importance of relationships and why this is important. If you're doing it right, even if you are building on the side you are still showing up fully at your day job. Again, the best way to success is by helping someone else build something. The relationship that you create in doing this will compound interest even long after you have departed that business. More than anything, make an effort to do right by people, and try to minimize the bridges you burn in business. I can't tell you how many of my former team members I've helped build their business and land their first clients. If you are working for a good leader they will want you to live in your passion, whether that's with them or not, and if you have showed up for them, when it's time they will help you. I've had former team members who literally built their businesses on the referrals I sent them, and have used that to take their business to another level.

You may be saving money or trying to create a plan to make a leap into entrepreneurship or to really expand the business you have started. Just know you may never feel completely comfortable, but if you make the leap a little more strategic you'll feel that much more at ease.

I like to sky dive but on my first attempt I went through hours of training, had a coach strapped to me to ensure I made the right moves, and a parachute for landing will require training. That as much as I love predictability will be unpredictable, but you have to be strategic.

4

Idea to Product: Building a Startup

Your biggest problem of the day should be how you are going to bridge the gap between where you are and where you want to be.

—Sevetri Wilson

There are many paths to take when starting a company. The two I continuously focus on in this book are: starting *with* funding and starting *without* funding. Each path from idea to product will look totally different because while some founders will have luxuries to begin with, others just won't.

Starting With Funding

If you start a company with funding you'll have money available to cover expenses such as engineers, marketing, and product development for a year or two at a minimum. This money can come from your personal account, a friends and family round, or outside investors.

In the case that you start your company *with* funding, you will have the luxury of being able to spend time on customer and product development. You'll be able to focus on:

1. Finding the problem(s)
2. Looking at potential solutions and interviewing customers about these solutions, hopefully using a mockup or quick prototype

3. Developing a minimal and viable product, and then consistently improving the product over time as customers are using it

Starting Without Funding

I would argue that your focal area when starting your company with little or no money is much different than if you did have money. Without funding, you need to focus on staying as lean as possible! As I discussed in my book *Solid Ground*, it's much easier to start with very little to no money if you have a services-based product that you can grow by way of contracts. That's how I started my first company, Solid Ground Innovations, a professional services agency. The path to growth was totally different than starting a tech company. In tech, unless you are a coder, you'll need to pay engineers and other developers early on to get a minimum viable product (MVP).

With little to no money, you must have a plan around sales and generating cash sooner rather than later. (This is the position of most companies.) In this case, where one of your main goals is to sell and get money through the door, I would suggest your focus look something like this:

1. Talking with a customer about their problem(s)
2. Discussing potential solutions and selling the customer on your solution
3. Getting money from the customer to deliver this solution to them (fast, not months later)
4. Building a solution (fast), licensing/finding another solution, or initially doing a concierge-type solution for the customer while building the automated product

At the end of the day, you can skip parts in building your company, regardless of whether it's with or without money, in order to scale growth. Too many founders get caught up in a lot of activities early on that do not immediately deliver sales and revenue.

If you have *some* funding, you have a *little* bit of the luxury of spending time on product development before making sales.

If you have *no* funding, you are forced to start generating revenue immediately. This isn't a bad thing, as it gets you to reality pretty quickly! A customer can say they "love" your product, but if they are not willing to fork out cash, then this is reality slapping you in the face.

What *Not* to Do When Starting a Company

The following points apply to most (but not all) startups that are just getting started. Trust me, I made a few of these mistakes myself early on. (Note: If you have *significant* funding, they won't apply as much.)

- Do *not* spend money on expensive lawyers (although never get into a contract agreement without some legal insight).
- Do *not* pay $10,000+ for a logo designer to figure out the look and feel of your brand. It's highly likely it'll change in the early days.
- Do *not* get an office. COVID-19 has made working from home a lot easier, but in the early days coffee shops or libraries worked just fine.
- Do *not* spend too much time "researching" in a theoretical way and too little time building the product or speaking with customers.
- Do *not* worry about your company structure (i.e. LLC, C corp, etc.). Resilia started as an LLC and eventually, as a part of our seed terms, reincorporated into a Delaware Corp.
- Do *not* worry about anything other than getting sales or building your MVP (minimum viable product).

You'll Never Get Going Unless . . .

When I say get early feedback, you want to figure out what kind of idea you have. There's a lot of work that has to happen to get an idea from your head to the shelf, so doing the early legwork and then executing it is going to be essential. You should find someone whose opinion you trust, ideally someone who is experienced in the area you are trying to dive into. If you tell your best friend, of course they are going to love it, but if they have no experience or barely know what you are talking about their feedback probably won't be useful. Use friends for moral support more than you use them to validate a business opportunity, unless they have the expertise to do so.

If you have a business idea, you are most likely looking to solve a problem. Right? Okay, make sure you answer in detail what that problem is.

Also, where did the idea come from? What prompted you to want to tackle this problem? Is it a problem you faced or noticed elsewhere? Is the issue solvable by tech? Is it a tech problem or an industry problem you feel can be solved by tech?

When collaborating, you'll want to know who else is out there doing this or solving this problem. Even if you believe no one is solving this problem, investors hate when founders say this because most likely someone is and you just haven't found them yet. So, don't fall into the trap that no one is out there doing this—do your research and get some competitive analysis. You don't have to create something that no one is doing, you have to create something that differentiates your product from your competition. So ask yourself some key questions, like why a customer might choose your brand or product over a competitor, especially if that competitor is already in the market. Do you bring better quality? Really hone in on what makes your solution different from what's out there. Try to be objective and ask yourself how you can commercialize your idea.

You are most likely very excited about the possibilities of your new idea, so keep that spirit, because the path to product and launch will no doubt at times remove that initial optimism.

You also want to think about what you want to accomplish in the near future and perhaps over time. Since it's just an idea, you'll probably know less about what five years out looks like, but trust me, people are going to ask eventually.

Because ideas can come from something you heard on your daily walk or you saw something very subtle and it sparked something in your head, you may think "I can't believe no one has done this before." You may think no one shares similar passions as you but what's more commonly true is that people may not have the time or money to execute on their idea. This is why I always say that what matters is not the person with the idea, it's the person who can execute it. If you watched the movie *The Social Network*, loosely based on the rise of Mark Zuckerberg, or any of the court documents related to where the original idea for Facebook came from, then you know this all too well.

You'll want to zone in on your idea and be clear about where the idea came from. You believe there's an opportunity in the market for your idea, and you are confident it is solving some problem. Or if your idea is a niche solution, or a luxury item where only a small subset of people would use it, you are fine with that.

Then you'll want to ask yourself a few other questions:

- Can you bring your idea to life (i.e. can you build it)?
- What is your internal mission? What is driving you?
- Do you want to find a co-founder or a partner to build this? (My personal experience is that the further you get down the road, the more resources you cough up alone, the harder it becomes to find a co-founder.)
- If not a co-founder, who else do you know who might help you bring your idea to life?

- Do you really want to start and run a company?
- Will you (eventually) quit your current job or profession to work on your idea full-time?

Next you'll want to understand what it will cost or what you can afford to invest to get your idea off the ground. At the end of the day, getting ideas off the ground really comes down to time, money, expertise, and execution. So, you have to really be honest with yourself about this. You can ask yourself some questions regarding this:

- Do you have any expertise that sets you apart to bring your business idea to life? Could you lead a talk on it ?
- What other skills can you bring to the table? Are you good at sales? At marketing?
- Do you understand what you do not know, what is beyond your own capabilities?
- What is missing and what needs to be filled immediately to get your idea to product?
- Do you have access to designers and other professionals?

When you think about the role that time plays, ask yourself whether, if you could be doing anything else, would you still be doing this? This is where you have to eliminate other factors. You really are your first project manager and timekeeper. No one is going to hold your feet to the fire.

- How much time can you dedicate to this idea . . . Daily?
- What current commitments do you have that will be there no matter what (i.e. family, caring for a sick relative)?

The last factor is money. The cost to take an idea to product runs the gambit, and really depends on what you want to invest to get the idea off the ground. Yes, you could go out and raise money, but the likelihood that you have zero personal investment into your idea early on is just really rare. Here are some questions you can ask yourself:

- Have I scoped out what it will cost me to get to a minimal viable product?
- Have I considered basic fees, such as incorporating my idea into a company?
- What are my associated costs to launching a website (if I'm not the designer) and other potential early needs?
- Most importantly, am I committed to making the investment and willing to fork over more time, if needed, or find investment resources elsewhere?

With anything that's going to take a considerable amount of time and alter your daily life, you have to consider everything that will be at work. Allowing yourself to answer some of these questions early on will alleviate some self-imposed stressors that come from just not knowing, or from not asking the right questions.

5 Building a Team

Entrepreneurs ask me what's one of the hardest parts of running a business and I always respond, hiring.

—Sevetri Wilson

Hiring and Finding Freelancers and Others

I've had some major wins with hiring. Those individuals I remember the most, their strengths, weaknesses, how we interacted and worked best together. What they brought to the team, the extra effort, the long hours, the willingness to step up when needed. So many different things made the individuals extraordinary at their roles respectfully. Yet, I'll also remember every time I got it wrong and why. Not a culture fit, the individual may have embellished their experience and couldn't perform once the time was needed, they doubted their work more than they should have. They stopped showing up not physically but they mentally clocked out and were not focused or perhaps they felt some work was beneath and was always waiting on someone else to do the job. Hiring is difficult yet, ultimately it will depend on your skills at (x) finding and (y) managing each type of resource. When people ask me what challenged me most early on, I say it was hiring. Hiring is hard. Over time it gets slightly easier, but not much.

When I hear from early-stage founders it's often to get my opinion on outsourcing various roles for their company, and if the founder is non-technical (meaning they can't themselves code or build their product), the question is always how I found engineers in lieu of having a CTO or hiring someone full-time. How do you get a freelancer or contractor to fully "buy in"?

In an ideal world, you'd get the cost-saving benefits of outsourcing along with the eagerness and real-time collaboration you get with a full-time hire sitting next to you, but in reality that combination hardly exists.

Generally, whoever is managing development at your company has experience in one of the two areas more than the other. If they are actually good at, and experienced with, managing a team in say, Ukraine (which is where we outsourced dev at one point), then it will probably work great. If they've never done this, but are instead used to working with a hands-on team in Austin, then outsourcing to Ukraine will almost certainly fail. I was fortunate that our first outsourced hire was able to oversee and communicate with an offshore team. Yet, this isn't always the case.

Ultimately, you'll need to find a way to manage both types of resources effectively.

After wasting tens of thousands of dollars on a dev shop, I was introduced to a technical consultant who had experience working with offshore teams. Our technical consultant helped source and oversee our offshore teams, first in Ukraine and then Pakistan. This saved me a ton of money, as I in many ways had the best of both worlds. I think one of the biggest mistakes founders make early on is trying to go offshore and hire developers when they have never managed offshore developers or, even worse, they aren't themselves technical. It's literally a recipe for disaster. Additionally, if you aren't technical it becomes hard to manage a developer in general. By hiring a technical consultant who worked for me, my offshore team was held accountable because the consultant reported back to me, and not the dev shop.

How can I hire great freelance talent over mediocre ones?

There are several methods that can help you find the right freelancer for your project.

One is to use a curated talent platform. There are plenty out there now, like Toptal and Andela, that have refined processes to offer a reliable, high-quality, and fast method of hiring top freelancers (Toptal only accepts the top 3% of candidates into their talent network). Yet, they can still be very expensive depending on how early you are in starting your business and how many resources you have. At one point we used Andela, but if I'm being frank I believe they had problems maintaining costs as they scaled. Thus, outsourcing through a talent platform with offices in the United States who then outsourced to Africa no longer made sense for us. I thoroughly enjoyed working with our engineer in Kenya who was also a Black woman and was amazing, but it became cost prohibitive and no longer truly made economic sense. From there we outsourced to Pakistan before bringing our entire dev team in house.

What are the pros and cons?

If you're short on time, curated talent platforms can access their network of freelancers, so that you will have just a select few candidates to interview and hire. In many ways they are like a recruiting firm.

Though Toptal offers a no-risk trial period, I am inclined to say that there is no such thing as no risk. Yet, the option allows you to hire a freelancer for your project and pay only if you're completely satisfied with your freelancer's work at the end of the trial period.

The other key item with platforms like this is pricing transparency. For the most part, you know what you get.

Referrals are another way to hire freelancers. If you don't have a trusted network who can recommend freelancers they have worked with or have been referred, then you can begin to build one. There are tons of slack channels and Facebook groups of tech people coming together to share resources and information; seek them out and join them.

What are the pros and cons?

The difficulty of pursuing this method lies in the need to (1) possess your own network of talented freelancers, and (2) attract these freelancers to your project. A great freelancer usually has their pick of projects, which means you may need to offer a higher pay rate or more scheduling flexibility if free-lancers are not immediately interested in your project.

Use an agency. If you go this route, you'll have to conduct your due diligence by reading reviews and speaking with each agency, of which there are many. What are the pros/cons? Well, I went the agency route at first and though we were able to get a minimal viable product (MVP) out of it, it's not a long-term solution. It's also going to cost you more than a freelancer because you are hiring a "one-stop shop" to get your product or MVP off the ground. Also note that agencies tend to be less flexible with their working style.

On the plus side, the pricing will be transparent up front for your project needs and the time it will take, though it may shift based on sprints to finish.

Though I've used a combination of these, what I've found is that freelancers recommended by friends or colleagues were almost always the best. What I've also found is that everyone has a different way of doing things. In time. if you hire a CTO or bring on a technical founder they may want to go an entirely different route, which can lead to rebuilding the entire infrastructure of your product if the CTO finds gaps or that engineers took shortcuts for the sake of getting a product to market.

GOING OFFSHORE

Pros

The number-one attraction is the cost of manpower. It's very cheap. That's why most try and some are able to go offshore successfully while others fail miserably.

Cons

You have no control over how many folks are working on your project or how experienced they are. The contractor may slide extra developers in and out of the project when it suits them, which may not be a big deal, but if you had a lead who knew a lot about the requirements, implementation, and architecture of your project and the offshore contractor needs them elsewhere, they may (transparently or not) slide out of the project for a little while, or forever, to assist with other projects that need help—*you don't have any control over that*, but there is a good chance that will happen.

I was pretty particular about staying with the same engineer throughout the duration of the work, and the only instance where this was not the case was when the engineer left the company I was working with. If you are presented with this dilemma, always push back to keep the same engineer working on your project (if the engineer is good).

Key features or QA strategies may be ignored completely, if the contractor falls behind schedule. I have experienced this, and because the agreement or contract made by management was not ironclad, the contractors got away with ditching some activities and features the company wanted.

Additionally, if you aren't a technical founder you are 10 times more likely to get screwed over because you don't know what you don't know. This is another reason why I hired a technical consultant—to ensure that I wasn't making these missteps along the way, which I wouldn't have been able to spot.

Side note: It's extremely difficult for nontechnical founders to raise money, but I believe there are ways to navigate until you find a full-time CTO if you are a solo founder, which is what I did. If you have found a CTO who can be a co-founder, a lot of this won't really apply unless they aren't fully bought in. In that case, you don't really have a co-founder.

Working with contractors may also be difficult because they may take a passive-aggressive posture, which means you need to have someone appointed to do what they said they would do (and agree to work with, transparently, the onshore client development team). You need a manager, or management team, that backs up their offshore team, especially if the goal is to relinquish the further development and maintenance of your product being created offshore.

Some offshore contractors may not want to make it easy to end or let go of the project. It is not in their interest to give that up, and they will probably hold on to control of that project until the customer ends the contract. Also watch out for contractors who may look for excuses to not keep up their end of the agreement (the project is behind schedule, it costs too much, etc.).

Things to improve the situation:

- Have an ironclad agreement in place: I am not an attorney, but it is very important to have everything in writing and signed; this ensures that it's not so easy for the contractor to slide out of things they agreed to do. My technical consultant was really good at helping ensure that everyone remembered what we agreed to do long after we had agreed to it, and continuously as we built. This was also important because I had someone who could create a checks and balances between the company and our developers since I myself am not technical.

- Expect transparency: Make it clear up front that you don't want to just wing it, and that you care about deadlines and quality control as well as transferring knowledge to your onshore in-house development team once that time comes. Schedule daily scrums and meetings with management on a weekly basis (communication will happen). Make it clear that there are consequences to not meeting deadlines, or throwing out QA, functional unit testing, and other agreed-upon items in the contract. Make sure they know the consequences of ignoring these required items. You can also set your contractors to be paid only after a sprint is completed, thus they are financially incentivized to do so.

- Create infrastructure: I believe that the reason we were able to use offshore developers for so long is that we created the infrastructure for them to be able to work within, such as cloud allocation, servers, and so on. Also, ensure they are trained on how to properly deliver completed work. If you work with an offshore team that has a management system in place, they will generally prioritize this as apart of their own built-in infrastructure.

- Always communicate: We communicated often via Slack, but early on our technical consultant also had standing calls/check-ins with our offshore team. Using a daily scrum format every work cycle, day or night (there may be a 15-hour time difference!), may mean that you have to do this at 10 p.m. or 6 or 7 a.m. All the offshore developers will briefly need to tell you (1) what they worked on yesterday (last time cycle), (2) what they plan on working on next, and (3) any impediments that they may have. We had weekly dev calls in which we were able to build rapport with our offshore team. They felt like—and were—an extension of our team, which made them (in my opinion) more accountable for the work they were doing.

- Have a detailed exit strategy: Everyone from my technical consultant to our offshore team knew a day would come when we'd likely transition. We made this clear up front, so that there would be no issues, and if you are working with a credible offshore team there shouldn't be any issues. In our case we brought on a CTO who would be responsible for leading our technical team. Because of this we had no issues with transitioning our offshore team off the work, and having them help with bringing full-time engineers up to speed on the work that we were doing.

I hear offshore horror stories, and I've had a bump in the road or two and understand how this can happen. Founders ask me "What if they just aren't doing what you asked?" I'd say that how a project starts is usually how it will finish, so you'll need to realign quickly and if there is no immediate change, then you should move on. Find another contractor or someone else who can take over the work. If you are close to launching a product or an important feature, then this is where you need to revisit your contract and what you agreed upon. Unfortunately, you'll likely have to just bite the bullet until you can bring another contractor up to speed and transition over.

One of the downsides to temporary offshore teams is that when you do hire full-time dev they will most likely run into problems where the application feels a bit buggy, or some temporary fixes were implemented that, while getting the job done, will need to be fixed for the long term.

At the end of the day, working with offshore teams doesn't have to be a bad experience. It really is all in how the relationship is handled, how the work starts (minus the time difference, it can be just like working with contractors in the United States, as a lot of this information is transferable), and picking the right team. And remember, if it's not working out, pivot quickly if you can.

Out of the Gate

When I first started hiring back during the SGI days I made tons of missteps. I had never hired anyone before and for some reason I never sought out someone to give me advice or coach me along the way early on. Yes, I had read a few management books, but I don't think anything really prepares you for managing people for the first time.

One thing I learned pretty quickly about myself is that I needed to run a hiring process that included the final decision-maker being more than just me and my thoughts about a candidate.

You can sometimes fall so in love with the idea of a candidate that you romanticize not only the position but the person in the position because having the ideal candidate would be a game changer. So you tell yourself that if only you can find this person then you'd be able to do X, Y, Z, and whew wouldn't that be nice.

So, a candidate sits across the table from you and they say all the right things. That's why it's important to run a hiring process that includes having enough people who know what you are looking for to have spoken with the candidate.

Hiring costs you time and money, and when employee turnovers happen early on in their time at the company, it costs you even more.

A candidate doesn't have to have everything on the first day, but they need to show the ability to grow within their role and within the company. Additionally, it's also on you to ensure that they have what they need to do this, within reason. If you are working in a startup then you should expect to work with limited resources; this is why it's so important to find people with grit.

With hires, you are trying to get it right the first time. We wish we could be so lucky that this will always be the case. You just won't get it right every time. Yet, usually within a short period of time you know when it's not right. One thing I've learned is that when you know it's time, let that person go. And if you're anything like me, an empath at heart, then this decision won't be easy. But trust me, it will save you a lot of time, money, and setbacks the quicker you rip the Band-Aid off. And it's probably best for both of you. You don't want someone in a place where they aren't excelling and have to look over their shoulder because they feel the hammer can come down at any moment. Sometimes it's just not a good fit and that's okay. This isn't to say that you shouldn't give promising team members the room to course correct; you should have to have discernment to know the difference.

There are best practices and techniques that will allow you to become a better hiring manager. Not everything has to be a trial-and-error type of experience, as too many mistakes early on can cost you your business.

Recruiting is hard. But it's one of the top jobs you will have as your company grows. So, as our company grew and the positions became more demanding and we had the need to recruit higher-stakes candidates, we moved to hire a recruiter.

A recruiter brings the ability to source much faster through a vetted and sourced network. They work with you to create the right profile and the specifications of the job as well as a detailed background on the company they use to source candidates with.

We also use LinkedIn Recruiter because there have been numerous times that we hired a recruiter to help source for us, but then someone within our network, even one of our own team members, referred someone we ultimately hired.

Yet, I still believe in hiring external recruiters when you can afford to, especially as you scale and it becomes critical that you source rock star candidates in key roles. You do still have to be very active in the process even though you have a recruiter on board. This means responding promptly to requests and getting candidates scheduled. Usually recruiters charge either anywhere between 10% and 20% of the candidate's first-year salary or a base price.

There are two different types of recruiters: contingency or retained.

We've used both.

Contingency versus Retained Recruiters

There are two types of contingency searches and generally two types of retained searches as well. There are contingency recruiters that are exclusive, meaning that the assignment has been given to a sole agency and won't involve payment until a candidate is actually placed. Then there are nonexclusive contingency recruiters, which means you are shopping around and likely have other recruiting agencies doing the search as well. There is also no payment involved until the candidate is placed.

There are also two types of retained recruitment agencies. There is the standard retained recruiter, which usually involves two payments: a standard fee to engage and another payment once the candidate is found. Then there is the engagement fee retained recruiter. This one you should be mindful of because the agency receives a portion of the fee up front and it's not refundable if you were to stop the search or find a candidate via a means other than the agency.

We've used both types of agencies and have paid upwards of $25,000 to secure a VP or higher in retained recruitment agencies. We found our C-suite recruiter via a recommendation. He had just left a larger firm where he had placed hundreds of people, and was venturing off to start his own agency. We were able to get him for half the usual price because of this, but he came with all the knowledge, tools, and resources to effectively recruit like a top-tier agency. For team members at the management or director level, this number was considerably lower. Yet, the numbers fluctuate significantly depending on the company you use, and their track record.

Another consideration, once you can afford it, is bringing your recruiter in-house. Matt Roberge, author of *The Sales Automation Formula* (Wiley, 2015), is a fan of this method. Instead of hiring a recruiter, he made an offer to bring the recruiter in-house, promising that the company would be much more successful this way. At Resilia, we'll hire our first Director of People Ops in 2021, who will also be responsible for managing, hiring, and further building out of culture at the company.

If you do not have the ability to hire a recruiter, turn LinkedIn into your personal recruiter, free of charge.

It's one of the most powerful tools I've found for hiring because you can use the search engine to source candidates by their current position, company, and other relevant facts.

Say you are looking for a salesperson. You can search companies that might align to yours, and give someone in a later-stage company than yours an opportunity to use the skills they gained to help a company that's earlier stage and have the opportunity for upside that might be unattainable in their current role. You can also see relevant activity of the candidate and glean some insights on whether you want to reach out and engage. If you do, then you can contact them via LinkedIn.

Because of COVID-19, the talent pool got much wider due to layoffs across the tech sector and in nearly every industry. The general rule of thumb that the best candidates aren't looking for job opportunities isn't necessarily true now, because candidates were getting let go not because of performance but because of steep cuts. I have a friend who had just left a great job he had been in for the past five years for an opportunity at a very-well-known tech company in January of 2020, and within just three months at his new job he, along with the majority of his HR department, lost his job.

Yet, regardless of the times you're still looking at high-performing individuals who are potentially looking for a challenge, a new opportunity to work with a start-up and one driven by a mission that they can be proud to say they are a part of.

At some point, particularly with millennials, people want to work at a company that is striving to have a greater impact and to create lasting human connections. Thus, our mission has helped us recruit talent from other companies and because of this our ratio of closing candidates is very high.

Once you've made the hire, now you have to take a candidate through onboarding.

It is said that a candidate knows within the first weeks or months whether they want to stay at a company. This is in large part due to their onboarding experience. We have spent time crafting our onboarding experience and, since we are an early startup, continue to iterate on this process. We also ask our new hires to give feedback on their experience, as it's important for us to build a culture where people feel that they can speak up.

The onboarding process is about integrating a new employee into our company and our culture as well as ensuring that the new hire has the tools and key information needed to thrive in their role. Yes, it includes things like getting a computer and joining Asana, Slack, and other systems of record, but it also means doing deep dives with team members across the company.

As soon as a new hire receives an offer letter and accepts, we begin to onboard them via an online portal with Justworks. If you aren't familiar with Justworks, it's a platform that helps employers manage payroll, benefits, employee information, and employment-related compliance. Here they can immediately discover information designed to engage them around the company.

As I mentioned, my very first full-time hire ever was in 2010, which means I've now been consistently hiring full-time people for over 10 years. My first hire wasn't an assistant, although sometimes I feel that people default to hiring an assistant as their first hire, and this might be an extreme need for many. For me, hiring someone I referred to as a generalist, someone who could wear multiple hats and was a logistics dream, was my first hire. I also broke one of my rules: let your friends stay your friends; don't hire them unless they are superb and bring proven skills to the table in a needed role. My first hire was one of my best friends, Shayla. Yet, I had worked with her through my sorority in college, I had lived with her as roommates, I had depended on her as a friend. So, when it came time to start my company she was the first person I thought about. She was in with no hesitation. At this time, we were both in grad school but we took the challenge full on.

We'd go on to grow Solid Ground pretty significantly in a short period of time. Not bad for two first-generation college students who had always been self-starters. After several years, she'd move on, going back to school to become a social worker and a photographer, proving that where you start doesn't always have to be your long-term trajectory. I cheered her on, as I do any of my team members who depart the company. It is without a doubt that I want those around me to do work they love and to live out their life as they imagine it.

While I was writing this book, I received a text from Shayla out of the blue. It said, "I've been wanting to say it for a while— thank you for all the opportunities that you have sent my way over the years. I hope you are well, my friend."

Managing teams, hiring, firing—none of it really gets easier but you do get better at it. If you want to run a successful company, you *must* get better at it.

Get Out of the Way

Now that you've hired these competent, capable people to help run parts of your company, it's time to get out of the way.

You really need to rely on your team to take on the work that you've hired them to do. As your company grows, you just don't have time for it.

You also have to learn to rely on them to make decisions in an early-stage startup.

Early on, you'll likely be the person with the most context on the business and as a result, you'll tend to be involved in almost all decisions, but when you're larger, you can no longer know everything about everything.

You need to shift from always being in the know about every single detail to enabling others to make decisions. I'll admit that this was an interesting adjustment for me in the early days. I knew virtually everything that was happening across the business at Solid Ground and when I started Resilia.

Yet, once you have so much going on at such high velocity that no one person can really stay on top of it all, especially as you are now hiring key leaders who are experts in their space, you aren't always in the best place to recommend the best course of action on certain topics for the business. So what do you do to teach yourself to delegate not only work but decision-making to the people you are hiring?

As the founder, you probably still have the best information and perspective on the company, and, yes, it is still important to connect all the dots. So, your role is to have context across the various parts of the company, which is an important role of the CEO, but you have to effectively push that context down to others, so that they can make informed decisions that are right for the company.

Once we started hiring senior leadership I really tried to hone in on this, but starting it even earlier can avoid a bottleneck, severely limiting your company's ability, as you continue to grow.

At the onset of COVID-19 things were evolving very quickly on a national and global scale and, like most companies, we had to make a series of critical decisions for our business and our employees. We have two offices; one we had just opened in January of 2020. Today, our team is still working remotely, though we don't suspect it will be permanent. The role of each managing team member is more important than ever now. They are responsible for those who report up to them and they also have to understand how their team feels, what's causing issues for them within (or outside) of the company, and how to resolve problems where feasible.

Managers are usually empowered by someone on the senior leadership team who is communicating their vision and expectations and working to keep things on course. Yet, their role isn't to micromanage.

This is why it's important to empower your team to make decisions, build a culture of trust, and explicitly let members on your team make decisions on behalf of the company. Create clear expectations so they know which decisions should be elevated to leadership for approval, and facilitate cross-functional collaboration to avoid dysfunctional silos where all decisions that span two or more functions get elevated to you; instead, I try to ensure that folks have the right information to make these decisions. You can continue on other work and focus on thoughtful communication to make sure that everybody's on the same page. That brings me to our next topic: the way you communicate changes a lot as you scale.

Earlier-stage relationships are close enough that it's easier at this stage, but this changes as your company grows; people have different perspectives from their individual experiences in areas of the business. They have different priorities, and they digest and understand information in dramatically different ways. Someone once told me that if you want folks to remember something you have to tell them five times in five different ways. I think that's a great way to think about it in a larger company; communication may not be as straightforward. The principles of communication remain the same as you grow. You have to be thoughtful about what and when you communicate and the implications of those decisions. Everyone likes to talk about transparency; transparency is important, but one of the things that folks talk about less is the timing of that transparency and how communications are rolled out. I don't like to spring anything that's a surprise on my team without a well-thought-out plan and the objective of the follow-on message. My CTO definitely holds my feet to the fire on this one. I'll run something by him and he'll suggest perhaps a different tone. If you know my personality then you know I'm a straight shooter, and I often don't mince words. Most of you might say, "well, that sounds right to me!" But as your team grows, if you want to retain talent you have to constantly check your tone and ensure that your approach isn't abrasive in a way that's offensive.

Transparency changes as you scale and grow because you have to be more thoughtful about how information cascades throughout your organization.

This helps equip your senior leadership to respond appropriately themselves and be prepared to answer any questions that come up if managers have questions or concerns.

It gives you time to make sure they're well informed and bought into whatever you're rolling out. I think effective transparency has four key characteristics:

> First, your communication should be timely. You might have the right message, but if your timing is off and you share important information with your team too late, you can come across as reactive on the flip side. If you talk about something too early, you can cause a huge amount of disruption, uncertainty, and speculation in your organization that distracts the team from keeping the business moving forward.

> Second, your communication should be strategic; always focus on why you're making this change, how it supports your strategy, how it will help you and your team achieve your mission, and strategize to build buy-in over time rather than expecting immediate adoption.

Something we are trying to work on is when we have a series of updates coming out across multiple channels, to help people and keep them posted in advance of the changes being rolled out. Expressing clear instructions on where to go with questions is important.

Third, your communication should be shareable. What I mean by this is that the messaging should be clear and easy to follow without room for misinterpretation or guesswork. It should also be as concise as possible. As your team grows, consider communicating using different channels. I mentioned earlier to leverage your management structure to cascade information. For us, this means making use of our internal content-sharing platform as well as Slack and highlighting important messages and weekly news updates, as well as covering them in our All Hands, which consists of everyone on our team.We make room for discussion in all of our All Hands and embed a Q&A document just in case someone doesn't feel comfortable asking a question in front of the entire team, but wants the question addressed during the team meeting as there might be others with the same question.

Finally, your communication should be actionable. If you're expecting your team to react in a certain way or with a specific set of actions, make sure that it's abundantly clear if there's a way for them to contribute and ways they can do so.

Let your team know how the information you share with them will impact them, what questions you have of them, and how they can contribute. This could mean keeping an eye out for further information, setting aside a time on their calendars for training, or providing feedback on an important topic.

6

I Hear You, But
I Need Capital

*When you fund Black founders, you help create
systemic, generational change.*
—Jewel Burks Solomon

More and more founders and entrepreneurs seem to be raising money from investors today than even when I first started raising capital back in 2015, especially Black, Latinx, and Women founders who have historically been underrepresented. We've seen a slight increase in the number of these founders who are successful in their pursuits, but that's still a far cry from what white male founders raise. In a recent report from Project Diane it found the Black women only received 0.27% of total venture capital investment between 2018 and 2019. One of the core reasons why people go out to fundraise is to bring big ideas to life faster and at scale. Yet, money isn't the only reason to raise capital; it's also about accessing people and resources from those that bring capital into your startup. Investors bring their networks and the introductions that you receive via these networks can help scale your company.

The first route most take (and try to omit) is a friends-and-family round. When we look at the disparity of funding, it makes perfect sense why people would try and skip this round. A lot of people don't have friends and family who can fork over $10,000 or more to help you with your idea, even if they think you're great and might succeed. In the next few chapters, I'll discuss how I went about raising each of my rounds. From my friends-and-family round to my latest Series A, now having raised $11 million for my startup, let me tell you—it's no easy feat, and from the point you start raising, you're always (kinda) in fundraising mode.

But before you start, there's some important terminology you should make yourself comfortable with.

Financing Terminology

There are a lot of things that you need to know about raising capital ahead of taking the leap. There's a lot of financial terminology and jargon that can trip up entrepreneurs who raise capital for the first or second time as investors ask for change. Many founders don't have a background in raising venture capital or even smaller angel rounds of investment.

For some, terms like pre-money versus post-money valuation might seem obvious, but for those who have never heard these terms, not so much.

The valuation of your company is really critical. Pre-money refers to your company's value before your next round of financing. Let's say an investor is seeking to invest in your startup. You and the investor come to an agreement that the company is worth $5 million and the investor will put in $250,000.

The percentage of ownership will be determined on whether the valuation ($5 million) is pre-money or post-money. If the $5 million valuation takes into account the $250,000 investment, then it is post-money.

These terms are important because they determine the equity stake you'll give up in your company.

Let's consider another example. Say the company was valued at $2 million pre-money and the investor put in $500,000, which brings the total to $2,500,000. The percentage that the investor owns of the company is 20%, because the valuation of the company was $2 million before the investment.

If the $2 million valuation is post-money and the investor puts in $500,000, then the current value is $1,500,000 and the investment of $500,000 puts the company at a $2 million valuation, which means the investor's ownership in the company is 25%.

You can see how important it is to clarify between pre- and post-money valuations when discussing investment terms. I'll talk a little bit more about legal vehicles in the future, but when we went off to raise our first dollars we utilized a SAFE (discussed later).

When you are going out to raise money for the first time, unless your company is a hot startup that everyone is clawing to get at, be prepared for battle. It's not all horrible, but a lot of it is. There are moments of extreme joy but also deep lows. Deep, humbling lows. So, be prepared for what many would call a very painful process. Also, your first angel check might come very easily; it might also be very hard. I've seen many founders get their first investment check so easily that when they have to raise more capital from those not in their immediate circles, they are blindsided by just how hard this came to be.

One mistake I didn't make early on was setting a time limit to raise money. Because of this, I constantly felt like I was raising capital. Sometimes minority founders, Black and Brown founders, don't actually have the luxury of a short fundraising cycle. But if you can put everything into a timeline and be prepared to tackle diligence head-on, you'll be much more capable of actually shortening your fundraising timeline.

Seek out investors who truly believe in you. Early on this will mostly 100% be the case anyway because it's going to take someone who truly does believe in you to invest any type of money into your company.

You can also turn to the Glossary later in this book and make sure you are up to speed on some additional key startup terminology. As I noted earlier, a business and a startup can be very different. I remember just starting out and not knowing some of the lingo that investors and others were using. When it comes to contracts and legal documents, you'll need to know this stuff, so go check it out.

Preparing to Raise

The very first dollars into your company will likely come out of your own pocket. This belief isn't one that's shared by all, especially those who had the experience of investing thousands of dollars of their own financing back into their company, then later seeing other founders raise capital on an idea without having to make an initial investment of their own capital. But this is a luxury that most people reading this won't have.

Because of the success of my first company I was able to reinvest the first capital into Resilia. This was a risk. I was taking capital that could have been used for reinvestment into my current company and investing it into an idea. Some thought I was crazy and maybe I was. Why would I begin to build a new company when my current business was doing well? I was watching as technology continued to disrupt every sector around me, and I knew that either I was going to continue to be disrupted by it or become a disruptor. I chose the latter. But let me repeat: the first money into your startup for the majority of founders will likely come from your own pocket.

Unless you have a product that has a massive audience, traction, and is sought after by investors, if you need capital in a short few weeks or even months, you're already late. I've found that the founders who are most capable of raising capital for their startups are the ones who have built relationships with investors over a period of time. For me, this presented a problem because I was living in New Orleans. I don't think I have to explain to anyone that the source of capital for early-stage companies is very scarce in Louisiana. But when I felt I had at least a proof of concept, I started looking for angel investors at home. Then in 2016, I raised $400,000 in capital from angels who were all based in Louisiana. This was the first time I'd raised this type of money, and to be frank I'd never asked anyone for money, especially not for a startup; remember, my first business was bootstrapped. How did I do it? I'll talk about it more in a later chapter but again, it all goes back to relationships. The first dollars in your company will be from people who believe in *you* more than they believe in what you are building. They believe that you are the person to see this idea to fruition, and that if you don't they can rest assured that you gave it your all. At least this is the mindset of your ideal first investor.

Now I wasn't born with relationships. I'm a self-proclaimed ambivert. The extrovert in me knows that the key to success is largely due in part to relationships. Yes, you have to bring a lot to the table as well, but what often gets you a seat there is relationships. As a first-generation college student from a rural city, I had to build relationships organically. I had to put myself in position to meet people, and ask for the right things, and build a strong set of capabilities for which people would call upon me to execute certain things. Additionally, people like working with people that they like. I know it seems simplistic, but I don't know too many people in early-stage investing who are writing checks and sending wires to people they don't enjoy talking to or being around. Lastly, you have to be able to be able to sell yourself and know how to communicate your plan and that you are the right person to execute it.

What Legal Documents Should I Use?

Legal documents can vary from round to round. For Resilia, we used a simple agreement for future equity (SAFE). Others may use a convertible note.

In 2013, Y Combinator, one of the most well-known startup accelerators in the world, introduced their SAFE (simple agreement for future equity) for startups that went through its program, but non-YC startups adopted the instrument as their preferred vehicle for early fundraising, including the instrument I used for my first investment.

The reason they introduced the SAFE is because it was a simple and fast way to get those first checks into a company and to show that the holders of SAFEs were early investors into a future priced round. I used a pre-money SAFE but now with the changes in the size of rounds YC has updated its SAFEs to be post-money. You can find a more detailed description of pre-money and post-money in the Glossary of this book.

Ultimately, I decided to use a SAFE because it was easy and it also saves startups and investor money in legal fees.

I know I said don't spend a hefty amount on legal fees early on, but something you will absolutely need to get right is the legal paperwork surrounding your investors. You have to make sure you understand the basics of investment structures or you could be royally screwed. Particularly for founders who have never raised capital of any kind for a startup, this can be a hard road to navigate. How do you value your company? How much equity stake do you give up? You'll want to familiarize yourself with investor term sheets and letters of intent, essentially a proposed set of conditions connected with an investment in your startup. It can be as short as one page or continue for several pages, and most times (with a few exceptions) it's nonbinding.

When you are raising a small round from angels, it's normal for the founder to set the terms of the investment, usually with some legal guidance. When you are looking for a lead investor for a larger, more sizable investment or later round you will most likely negotiate a term sheet given to you by a lead investor. You'll want to consider a few provisions around a term sheet, including the investment structure. Angel investors usually invest in one of three types of securities: convertible preferred shares, convertible debt, or common shares. Convertible debt starts with angels loaning money to the company and then that amount is converted into equity shares. The primary upside to convertible debt is that parties can defer putting a valuation on the startup until a later financing round. When a later round is finished, the debt converts into equity shares at the purchase price and usually has a discount associated with the conversion that benefits the angel investor for coming in early. Common shares are issued as evidence of the money paid into the company. With both common and convertible preferred share transactions, the parties will set the price of the investment with a fixed valuation on the startup.

There are a few terms you'll need to know about quantifying the preferred return of the investment and quantifying any occurring earnings on the investment.

Next you'll want to focus on shareholder agreements, board structure, and reporting.

You'll want to establish regular, honest communication with your shareholders. Most startups face hardships but what I've found is that when you communicate regularly and your investors aren't taken by surprise, they are more likely to weather the storm on your side. This isn't to say that there will be no friction between you and your board. One thing I regret about building my own board is that I would have kept it smaller. Board size definitely ranges where some founders will not formalize a board that includes investors until their Series A raise especially if their Seed round was relatively small like ours ($2M).

I'd like to say that most angel investors are on your side if you choose them well, but we all know cases where this has not been the case.

Due diligence is a critical part of investment and tends to get more rigorous over time and as you raise more money.

So, what does diligence look like and how do you prepare for it?

As I mentioned earlier, most founders will have to have some proof of concept or traction when they go out and raise capital. So really take this into consideration and understand how to present your idea to investors. You'll need to properly convey your strengths and opportunities via a well-crafted pitch deck, which is one of the tools in the capital-raising toolkit you'll need, and probably the most obvious. I've already referenced it several times, and I've included a sample of my deck in the Appendix. If you have any decks, include information about your current customers, and if you do, be prepared for investors to ask to speak to a few of them. This will be a part of later-stage investing as I find that most early stage (pre-seed) investors don't check for this if you don't have customers, but be prepared if they do.

Another situation some founders can find themselves in is not fully knowing (or ignoring) their existing liabilities, such as tax liens or lawsuits that might make investors raise eyebrows and not follow through on the investment. This is more noteworthy in a seed ($2 million-plus) or Series A round. It's not a deal breaker but you'll want to disclose this information early if you aren't able to do clean up immediately. If you have intellectual property, great; present any patents, copyrights, or licenses you might have. Be sure to have corporate records and documents in order. You'll want to have all of your t's crossed and i's dotted by your seed round. This means being able to easily access contracts from both customers and/or vendors, leases, and your corporate filing. You'll have to present some form of your go-to-market strategy, so do research on your market size and opportunity. Have your organizational chart prepared, and explain your current headcount (even if it's just you), how you might use funding to expand your team, and if you are eyeing a specific requirement.

In summary, founders seeking angel investing need to understand the legal requirements surrounding the forthcoming investments into their startup. Key items include provisions, investment instruments, terms and conditions of the investment, governance, shareholder agreements, and due diligence.

The more founders are prepared for what's to come when they start raising money, the better off they are.

Here is a snapshot of a real diligence request I received from an investor when I went out to raise a seed round of financing. Now to frame this a bit, this was the most extensive diligence request compiled by an angel network of investors I have received. I'll give a quick story here and show why at some point you have to decide if the investment is worth the time you have to put into responding to the requests. Some investors do the most, and I do mean the most.

I went through a rigorous process and we responded to every single question. The diligence was broken down into various buckets; what I show are the tech/IP questions we were asked by the team that led this particular part of the diligence. We gave them everything, they spoke to customers, and several of our advisors (one of whom is the president at a Fortune 500 company), they gave rave reviews, and scheduled personal calls. And you know what? We didn't get the investment. The managing partner took the time to go through the feedback from the diligence with me, and he looked me in my eyes and said, "To be honest, I was surprised we didn't do the deal. You had everything there." He then chalked it up to bad timing, while laughing, I might add, because I just happened to be presenting the same night as a Series B company. So it wasn't that I didn't pitch well, and it wasn't that the partners and angels didn't believe it was a great company; they had just decided to make only one investment that night, and it wasn't my company. I couldn't help but think what a waste of my time the process was—the time of my very busy advisors and the time of my teams, who were taken through a grueling diligence process that they successful executed.

Here are just some of the questions from the actual diligence document. I've included every single diligence question I've ever received in a free downloadable document available at www.sevetriwilson.com/.

Note: We were still named Exempt Me Now at the time; we would rebrand to Resilia in January 2019.

Exempt Me Now Technology and Product Due Diligence

- Please set up an account for us to try using the product.
- Describe current technology stack and any changes planned for going forward.
- ERP system? Accounting system?
- Describe automation/integration between billing system and your accounting system.
- Show key processes used within EMN (e.g., to build Form 1023-EZ). Flow diagrams available?
- Expanded product and technology roadmaps:
    - Hours to complete all projects?
    - Current staff capable of completing these projects?
    - If not, how many new programmers are needed?
- PCI Compliance:
    - Estimate to be self-certified
    - Estimate to be Level 1 certified
- We will want to setup calls with:
    - (REDADTED)
- Send resumes for (REDACTED).
- Send employment agreements/contractor agreements for (REDATED).
- Who is the CTO?
    - Send resume.
    - If no CTO presently, do you have any candidates?
- Is software written for specific verticals? How easy is it to migrate for another topic/issue?
- Multi-language capable?
- Current bug list.
- Discuss testing and rollout plans for new versions.
- Current servers can handle how many customers?
- Any plans for template galleries for large enterprises for front-facing apps?
- What API/integration is already complete for customers?
- What plans are there for artificial intelligence?
- Is there a current Technology Committee?

- Who designed your website?
- Does the website have dynamic resizing?
- What CMS used for the website?
- How I/O intensive is the system and requirements?

I share this information so that if you do decide to raise capital, you're better prepared and so that you can truly understand the types of questions that might come your way. Do I feel that Black and women founders undergo a more grueling diligence process? One hundred percent! I know this because I've talked to my white male colleagues and they were floored by some of the questions I received at the earliest stage of the company.

The investor said it was surprising to him that we didn't get the investment—well, just imagine our faces! It was surprising to us as well. It can be hard to gauge which investors are worth the time to engage and which are really wasting your time. Sometimes you know but may be holding out with a sliver of faith they will come through, and other times you are taken off guard. Yet, I've found that in the long run not receiving the investment was the best thing that likely could have happened to me. All money isn't good money. When you see investors being bad actors go in the other direction.

Though you may think investors have all the leverage, I'd urge you to also make sure you ask the right questions of investors early on. The right questions early enough can save you headache, heartache, and lots of time. Sometimes we can romanticize raising capital in away that is detrimental to our process. If the investor is going to invest, you'll know; if they are truly interested in you as a founder or in the company, you'll know.

Running a fundraising process is like sales. You have to ask the right questions to validate the fit.

Here are some questions you should ask investors:

- What is your investment thesis? (Maybe their thesis is to invest in companies in the Southeast region or outside of Silicon Valley.)

- Do you lead rounds? (I know many founders who struggled to find their anchor or lead investor—it can be very hard getting that first check in—but when you do, it's much easier to fill out the rest of your round.)
- What type of companies do you typically invest in?
- Where are you within your fund's life cycle? (This lets you know if the fund was just raised or if it is close to being fully allocated.)
- Do you follow investments? (The later your round, the more important it is that you have investors who can follow on in future rounds of financing you take on for the company.)
- How many investments do you make a year? How many have you already made?

Some background diligence you should also consider is seeing what companies are in the investor's portfolio and reaching out to them via LinkedIn to hear directly from them about what their experience has been working with the investor. Taking on investment capital is like entering into a long marriage, with hopes that one day it will come to an amicable end with an IPO, exit, or some other event that leads to returns for the investors and the company.

7

Raising a Pre-Seed $400,000

Even if no one sees it for you, you have to see it for yourself.

—*Sevetri Wilson*

Pre-Seed, Better Known as a Friends-and-Family Round

I look back on my fundraising journey and all the hurdles I faced. I don't think then I really understood the gravity of what it meant for my earliest investors to take a bet on me. For them to realize their money could have went to zero, and for them to have invested in the company,into my ideas and aspirations anyway. Later investments become more aligned with milestones and monetary gain. Investors want a return and you are reminded of expectations of you to meet goals aligned with that result often at every turn. Even with this I held a great responsibility to those who invested in our friends and family round, and most importantly I wanted to show them that their investment wouldn't be in vain. A lot of the early fundraising success founders have is through their network.

Yet, many don't have the network or friends and family who can pitch in money to help them raise that first pre-seed round.

I didn't inherit a network at the beginning of my business career either, but over time, I built one. I was in a conversation where the individuals were discussing the value of a college education today, saying that they had found the most value in their careers outside of college. Yet, one of college's biggest values is building a network. When people are thinking about individuals who might have $5,000 to spare, they often tap into their college circle of friends or colleagues they have met via their college networks who can afford to invest in their company. I've watched as venture capitalists started entire funds off the backs of their MBA classmates and leveraged the network they had built. I raised the first $400,000 in small and large chunks that ranged from $10,000 up to $75,000. I also participated in a program called the New Orleans Startup Fund. They wrote a $20,000 check to the company and returned with another $50,000 in our seed round.

Today there has never been a better time to raise money because people are just so much better connected.

One thing I wish I had done differently was doing a better job of tracking my meetings early on. If someone agrees to take a meeting with you at this stage, they are at least interested and willing to hear you out. Even if they do not decide to invest at that very moment, it's important to make note of the encounter. Were they optimistic? Did they give you feedback? Do they need additional information? When at all possible, it's great to understand a person's reason for not investing, even if it's they just didn't have the finances to do so.

When raising the first dollars for your company it's important that you are telling a compelling story. I know this might seem obvious, but I feel a lot of people miss the mark here. A powerful narrative of how you came about this problem, and why you are the best person to solve it, is key. You have to make the person sitting across from you really believe in what you are pitching them, even if they don't clearly understand what the company does; early investors might not fully get it unless they have invested in other startups. As I mentioned before, they are investing in *you*.

Certainly if you are raising money with an idea, maybe you'll need a minimum viable product to craft your story. Then tell that story over and over until you have perfected it but ensure that it remains genuine and effective.

I also found it extremely helpful that I was a part of the story and narrative, too, so I wasn't just solving a problem for other people. I was solving a problem that existed for me, too.

I remember sitting across the table from one of my first investors. I had crafted a pitch deck, and gave it to him to review. I told him that I wanted to build a company that was targeting the philanthropic sector to streamline a lot of the processes and nuances that existed between vendors and grant makers because as a consultant I knew that there had to be a better way of doing things. Whether that was creating a more effective way to do evaluations of organizations, or bringing capacity support to organizations on demand through a software solution, I had worked closing with my target audience and made it clear that I knew their pain point.

This investor not only knew that I was passionate about the work, he had witnessed it via the work we had done together. He ultimately felt that I had a solution that could really solve a problem, but even more than that, he believed in me and felt I had delivered a compelling story and reason he should invest. He told me so. He told me, you know what has made me so successful in business? Not what you do, but the team you build and how you empower them around what you are seeking to build.

He told me that during his own business journey he had helped create 17 millionaires by way of just giving really smart people the opportunity to grow and innovate.

He felt that I had the leadership capabilities, the tenacity, and the audacity to do the same.

So, take a risk and be a part of your story. We are not robots; we don't have to be perfect; to the contrary, we have to be human and genuine. Tell your story, not just your company's, and let your passion and drive really show through, and most importantly, why you are best suited to build this company.

Investors know that most successful companies will change over time, so at this point they are investing in you as a founder even more than in the company. Investors believe you can solve this problem and that you're capable of building this company, and they're ready to make that bet because of this.

Don't get too caught up in a deck and being concerned about projections. These things are nice to have but they won't be the deciding factor when someone invests that first check, unless it's institutional capital.

It is important to actually have a deck because most people will ask for one, or something like it, that helps them visualize what it is you are seeking to do.

In it you are discussing your particular challenge and how your solution could potentially be a game-changer, and your deck condenses all of this into a comprehensive snapshot.

There are funds writing pre-seed checks, such as Precursor, First Round, and Homebrew, that will require a deeper level of connectivity and investor pitching, but this won't be how most founders get their first check. More money flowing in the venture capital space and all the headlines around that can be a distraction. Yes, there's more money and more people looking to invest, but the large majority of this money is going to later-stage companies.

During our pre-seed, though, we were working on a minimal viable product (MVP) that we had not launched into the market, but we still had something to show early investors.

Some founders will raise capital early to get to a MVP and that's fine too. But you'll still have to put in sweat equity to get to this point. Also note, the fundraising journey never really slows down. Once you take the first capital in, the expectation is that you'll continue to raise money to grow the company, as how else are investors supposed to get their multiple return?

We built our MVP and launched our first product into the market in November 2016.

Some of you will have to show a workable product to attract investors, even your earliest investor check. It can be an extremely bare bones version, but show some functionality, which was what we did for our MVP. To paraphrase Ismail, my technical consultant during this time, he would say that if your product doesn't have some bugs and error messages then you probably launched too late.

Additionally, we were consultants who were seeking to solve a problem in our space via technology and a software solution, so in many ways we already had our MVP. We just had to prove that our customers would now want the service via a tech-enabled platform.

We were also able to clearly define our market opportunity. Where we faced the largest hurdles was trying to convince investors of our market size. Over time, that would be less of a factor. Looking back from then to the present, it's amazing to think that now we have investors who reach out to us saying how they have been following the sector and they see the large opportunity that awaits us.

The reason we raised a pre-seed round was because we were starting to build out our product, and the engineering bills started to really add up. Additionally, we needed support in other areas and I certainly needed some, even if minimal, legal counseling. We still didn't have any full-time employees, only contractors, which is where the chapter regarding offshore talent and hiring comes into play.

I had already invested a significant amount of money into the company early on and would continue to do so as we continued to grow. Depending on what you are doing, $400,000 may seem like a lot of money, but it goes quickly when you're building a product and software, even if you stay lean.

Then there is a matter of building a team and convincing people to come work for you. This is also not always an easy feat this early on.

In your pre-seed round your check size tends to be small because of the early stage of your startup. If you are in need of capital, the way in which you are able to secure it is critical to the success of your startup. As I mentioned before, you will be challenged with convincing early investors to back your startup because at this stage most have little to no traction. Some people would call this the triple F round—friends, family, and fools. I mean, after all, for this round most founders don't have a product market fit or even a product, or if they do they are in the very early stages, where success can't be determined.

Founders can be a little hesitant to ask their friends and family for money, because what happens if the business fails? Here's the thing: most businesses do. I always tell founders to make sure early investors know the full risks of their investment. If your business were to fail and you couldn't return money, it'd be good to know that the person will still talk to you the next day. Sure, no one wants to lose money. That's why this early, investors are usually betting on you more than they are betting on your idea. They are betting that you are a capable and competent human being who will give it their all to see this company through. That's why, in the event you lose it all, they (hopefully) won't cut ties with you because you did just that—your best. Here are a few pointers when raising a friends-and-family round.

Doubling down on what I've already stated, be clear about the risks.

Mixing money and personal relationships can be risky, especially if things don't go as planned. If you want to ensure that your relationship stays intact no matter how your company ultimately does, your number-one responsibility is to be candid about the risks. At the end of the day, the risk that they are assuming is a high one; after all, nine out of 10 startups fail.

Yes, they could lose all of their money and because this isn't a loan, it's a solid loss. In fact, tell the individual that if they need the money for anything else that's critical or might make a request to have the money returned, then they shouldn't make the investment in you (or in anyone, to be honest).

The fact of the matter is, not only do nine out of 10 startups fail, one out of five startups fail in their first year, and more than half by their fifth year. After clarifying the risks, picking a sound fundraising strategy is what comes next, and please don't forget to ensure that any transactions or money you take is documented.

The Pitch

There are some ways to craft a pitch tailored to family and friends. A close relative might appreciate hearing about your idea in person, whereas a former colleague or friend might be fine with a call and a follow-up email. Clearly and succinctly state your idea, why you are the right person to build, and why there is no better time than now to tackle your market.

Either way, the initial conversation can be hard to frame, so here are some conversation tips:

- Invest only if you can afford to lose this money. If you need it for anything important or think you might need to cash out quickly, this isn't the right investment for you.
- If you are interested, I will tell you more about my vision, goals, and milestones, and be candid about the challenges I'm likely to face.
- If you decide to invest, I will be sending regular updates on our progress, along with other investors, via email. *Side note:* When I wasn't in constant contact with my investors outside of email, I would schedule a dial-in phone conversation by Zoom or Google hangouts for

investors to get updates and ask questions; I found that hearing your voice goes a long way.

- If you have relevant experience, I would love to create a relationship to get your advice as we build this company.
- Though your investment won't give you a say into how I run the company, it will help guide my thoughts and decisions.
- Your support means the world to me and I will work as hard as I can to succeed and deliver a good outcome to all of my investors.

Setting expectations early on is key, although I feel this is something every founder has their ups and downs with, including myself. After you've gotten some interest, a major question that comes up is how much you should try and educate your friends and family on what you are doing. Sometimes very early investors can be unfamiliar with business and startups if they haven't had experience in running one. I would personally keep it at a high level, describing key items such as opportunities, timelines, and key milestones and the team you hope to build. Yet, for someone who is a bit used to investing early and familiar with startups you'll want to have a more detailed plan of action. I found that having a plan for at least the first three years was a good way to go about this, ensuring I shared specific metrics and target revenue goals.

Next you'll want to manage involvement well. I was pretty lucky that I didn't have any issues with my investors wanting to help run the company, but I've definitely heard of some horror stories of investors trying to do just that. It's important to let investors know that they will get updates on a regular basis. You can set this tone very early by letting investors know whether the updates are every quarter (my preference) or every month; just be sure to keep that schedule, as not hearing from you as planned might raise red flags. It's important to manage expectations, as these are your first investors and so they will likely be invested for a long time. Here's what your email could look like:

Subject: [company name] [month, year] update

Hi everyone.

It's been a great [quarter/month/etc.] here at [company name]. Since our last update, our focus has been on [thing 1], [thing 2], and [thing 3].

Key Results (or milestones):

- [key result 1, e.g., product advance]
- [key result 2, e.g., customer traction]
- [key result 3, e.g., financial milestone]

This month, we're focusing on [new focus]. Our goal is to [goal].

The biggest challenges we're dealing with right now are:

- [challenge 1, e.g., technical challenge]
- [challenge 2, e.g., competitor just raised money]
- [challenge 3, e.g., customer request you don't know how to address]

If you know anyone we should talk to about any of these issues, please reach out so that we can discuss further.

Best,

[your name]

Keep it really simple and make sure you bcc everyone, as you don't want back-and-forth responses. Don't try to beef up your achievements or minimize your challenges. Also, if your investors don't know how to help you, then they won't. Additionally, investors often won't respond to these emails even if they might help you, so if you know your investors have a special skill set, reach out to them directly and ask to schedule some time with them to see how they can help.

Don't turn friends and family into a crutch.

So, here's the thing. As a startup, especially one that starts down the path of raising money, it's inevitable that you'll need more, usually because you're either running out of money or because you are gaining traction.

There are other ways of raising money, such as crowdfunding. There are so many founders who have really knocked this out of the park.

If you need more money because you are gaining traction, it might be time to raise from more experienced investors and move into your seed round, but before I tell you how I raised a $2 million seed round, I want to discuss accelerators and pitch competitions as alternative means to get capital for your growing startup, the topic of the next chapter.

8

Accelerators and Pitch Competitions? Bang or Bust

I believe luck is preparation meeting opportunity.
If you hadn't been prepared when the opportunity
came along, you wouldn't have been lucky.

—*Oprah Winfrey*

Let's start with pitch competitions. I feel that the goal of pitch competitions has changed over the past few years—and not necessarily for the better. At one point, I felt that pitch competitions were held to position startups for opportunities to align with investors in their respective sectors. This is still the case in many instances, as it's still not uncommon to see winners of competitions like TechCrunch Disrupt go on to raise millions of dollars for their startup. The upside to pitch competitions is that their nondilutive capital (most times) allows an early startup the much-needed capital to continue to build out their minimal product, make that hire, or extend its overall runway. When you think about it, you can't really beat that, if you win. The downside to pitch competitions is that they can be less about who has the best idea or company and more about who has the best pitch. Judges often have very limited information related to the company they are judging, and they are making a decision based on a 3- to 10-minute pitch. Thus, whoever has the best crafted pitch is most likely going to win the competition. What I have also noticed about pitch competitions over the years is that they have been used as a way for large companies to boast their commitments to fund minority groups, and in many cases this has reduced pitch competitions to a parade of Black, Indigenous, people of color (POC), and women across stages for what amounts to pennies in comparison to the impact these large companies can have if they were to, say, create a fund for these same people and invest in their companies versus creating a stage where they must compete. I've been in two pitch competitions and I swore I'd never do a third, primarily because I weighed the time and cost associated with prepping for one, and for me it was not worth it.

The first pitch competition I participated in took place in upstate New York and was held by Chloe Capital, a new very-early-stage fund that was created to invest in women. After submitting my application and the pool being narrowed down, I was invited to pitch to a panel of investors in New York. Here's the thing: I had to pay my own way to get there and for housing and lodging. That's another thing about pitch competitions: you will usually have to pay out of pocket if you have to travel to various pitch events. The event took place over two days, with a welcome and Founder-meets-Investor type of dinner. I missed the first day of activities because my flight was delayed, which caused me to have to take a later flight—not really a big deal, but the airport shuffle had consumed my day, and nearly gave me an anxiety attack. Once I got there I met a group of female investors, all of whom were great, and I enjoyed listening to their stories along with learning about the ideas of the other startup founders. The next day was the pitch competition. Now this was my very first pitch competition, ever. We were in a room with invited investors who were there for angel investor training, along with the judges who would be hearing our pitches and making a selection. Prior to the pitch, we had a round robin of investor feedback regarding our startup and advice. Here is where I feel I failed. For very-early-stage founders and for someone like myself who was pitching for the first time, receiving feedback from four different investors about what I should and shouldn't say minutes before I gave my pitch was a recipe for disaster. I made the horrible mistake of trying to change my pitch on the fly to accommodate the investors' advice, and I failed miserably. The pitch was only three minutes; I don't know if you have ever had to try and communicate your company, products, traction, go-to-market strategy, and what you'd do with the investment within three minutes, but, to put it lightly, my pitch didn't go well. I know it was disappointing for the selection committee, who knew what our company looked like on paper, and were most likely dismayed I couldn't draw it out in my pitch. I did one of the worst things you can possibly do when giving a pitch: I didn't finish. Yes, that's right. I never got to the end, never revealed the grand finale, and was quickly reminded of this when the alarm sounded and the time monitor yelled, "Time's up!" I had traveled all the way to upstate New York by plane, train, *and* automobile. Needless to say, I felt deflated.

Here's what I would have done differently. First, I would have stuck with my original pitch. I would have listened to the advice of the other investors but stored it to decipher later. I would have also gone with my elevator pitch—you know, the shorter pitch you give to someone if you only have a short period of time with them. I would have honed in on delivering answers to two key questions: (1) Did I clearly communicate what the company is and how we make money? and (2) Was I able to sell them on one key problem that I was solving?

However, here's the thing about pitch competitions: even when you nail it you can still lose. Yes, I lost a pitch competition not just once, I've lost both pitch competitions I've ever competed in. The second one, however, I nailed! And I'm not just saying this—even today I still I run into people who tell me they remember my pitch.

In 2018, I was selected as one of three founders to pitch at New Orleans Entrepreneur Week. I knew the other founders fairly well, as the New Orleans tech scene is quite small. One was a dog dating app and the other a biotech company; I know, drastically different companies were competing. This time we had about 10 minutes to pitch. Perfect, I thought; I can definitely communicate my pitch in 10 minutes. Additionally, I had a day of practice with a speaking coach mentor of mine who would sign off on what I was saying. Was it compelling? Was it persuasive? Did I draw down on all the key elements of the company: team, market opportunity, traction, problem, and so on? I had it. One key difference this time was that it was the audience who selected the winner via a voting system. After I delivered likely the best pitch and speaking engagement I'd ever given, the voting commenced. I didn't win—again. Afterwards a number of founders approached me and said how they voted for me; others who didn't vote for me approached me and said they felt my startup was doing so well already that they couldn't imagine I'd need the money. Yes, I was penalized for having too much traction. I'd later learn that the winner of the competition was a professor at one of our local universities and gave extra credit to his students to attend the competition and vote for him.

That's why I say that pitch competitions are tricky. Sometimes the best startup wins and sometimes they don't, and "best" can be such a hard thing to calculate. What one judge or audience participant sees as best, another might see as something else.

I know that after these two stories many founders might think I'm opposed to startup competitions, but to the contrary, I always tell founders to do a value assessment and to be honest with themselves about what they need to do to prepare to win. Though they didn't work for me, I have founder friends who have the complete opposite story; some of them were literally able to build their first MVP and go to market by winning competition after competition. Hey, you never know, maybe if I had stuck with it I would have won the third or the fourth competition. I believe if given the opportunity and founders can see the benefit in competing, then why not?

Pitch competitions are one way to secure early-stage funding into your startup; another is through accelerator programs.

Accelerators, though targeted at mostly early-stage startups, are much different from pitch competitions. Most startups take part in accelerators for a specific time period, usually about three months. Accelerators do just what the name might suggest; during the period a founder is in an accelerator the goal is to accelerate the growth of their early-stage startup. This is done by way of advisors, an infusion of capital (usually around $100,000), and access to a vast network. Yet, not all accelerator programs are created the same. I've participated in two accelerator programs, though the second was for companies that were further along and most of those in our cohort had raised a seed round and had enough product traction that they could service customers. The first accelerator I participated in was Newark Venture Partners while I was raising my seed round and Engage, based in Atlanta, while I was raising my Series A round. There are so many accelerator programs out there that it will be critical for you to do your diligence and figure out which one is the best for you. Also, most accelerator programs are seeking a pretty hefty equity percentage for a fairly small investment. Know that depending on how far along you are, this can be negotiable depending on how much traction you have, which was the case for me both times, though you'll never hear the partners of the accelerators publicly say this. Yet, remember that anything in a closed room is up for negotiation. That doesn't mean you'll get everything or anything you want, but if you don't feel comfortable with something, don't go along with it; and this goes for anything you attempt to negotiate.

The two most well-known accelerator programs are Silicon Valley–based Y Combinator, which started back in 2005 in Boston, and TechStars, which was founded a year later in Colorado. It's estimated that 172 new accelerators were created in a 10-year span after Y Combinator was created, and that today that number has almost doubled in size. Back when we had just launched I applied to YC but was not accepted. I still have the email response from the CEO telling me that instead of worrying about applying to YC I should go find a co-founder. When I look back on it today, I think it was divine intervention that I wasn't accepted into YC, as my journey would have been significantly different and not necessarily in a good way.

Because there are so many to choose from, when determining if an accelerator is right for you it's important to analyze what you need to grow. For me, what attracted me to NVP and Engage was their limited partners (LPs). LPs are the investors who invested in the fund that is now seeking to invest in startups. Their LPs were made up of companies and organizations that fell within our core verticals.

Some of NVP and Engage's LPs included Delta Airlines, Cox Communications, AT&T, Invesco, Audible, and a slew of other for-profit and large foundations, which are all target customers for us. We can and have received direct introductions to sell and pitch to these LPs to do business with them.

There are some key opportunities when trying to decide whether your company should join an accelerator program. Some benefits include access to resources and support. Accelerator programs can provide you access to legal services, domain experts around go-to-market strategy, and pricing, product, and sales advice. Generally, these services are free to a startup, but, fair warning, free advice in the accelerator doesn't mean it will stay free. After a startup has "graduated" out of the program, those experts may come with a price tag if you decide to keep them on as consultants. The support that you receive also comes from other founders in your cohort who might be able to give you advice, or peer-to-peer mentorship, which can be valuable. The founder journey can be very lonely, so it's very important to have others around you who are also going through a similar experience.

You can also use this time to develop key startup assets such as a multi-year financial pro-forma, which will come in handy when you are looking to raise additional funding. Additionally, a founding team may lack certain skills that will be invaluable as the company grows. For me, I came mostly from a business background, growing what I viewed as a traditional company that was bootstrapped. Because of this I understood the basics of building a business, I understood how to close a customer, and I had an operational background from years of business experience. Yet, even though I had built a business that I grew to seven figures, it was much different from the business that I was building now. The mechanics of a startup are just that, different. The lingo is different as well. I had to shift my mindset from slow and steady wins the race, to accelerate and scale growth to capture market share while staying as lean as possible for as long as possible. Also, for the first time I had board members that I had to report to. Being around other founders who were a part of my cohort and who were building tech startups and dealing with similar issues as I was allowed me to be a part of a community.

Accelerators are also some of the first and perhaps even largest sources of capital in early startups out of the gate. Most accelerators invest about $100,000 (or less or more) into each cohort company for a stake in the company. I mentioned earlier that if you join an accelerator you're most likely looking at giving up a stake in your company in exchange for the benefits listed previously. The average equity stake is usually between 5% and 8%. I've been very fortunate—I had the traction to be able to negotiate this equity stake. This is important. If you are a startup that is being courted and/or you bring something to the table that strengthens the cohort pool and have traction, it's highly possible that you will be able to negotiate the equity stake you give an accelerator in exchange for the resources of the accelerator and the investment. Most accelerators will tell you that they won't negotiate, but behind closed doors, if they really want you to be a part of their cohort, they will. I find that most founders don't even ask or push the issue. For me,

8% or even 5% was far more than I was willing to give up at the time I entered each of the accelerators I participated in. I was also willing to walk away from the accelerator if they were unwilling to negotiate the equity stake in the company. Yet, this type of negotiation won't always work. There are several factors you should take into consideration, and those are: the stage of your company, how much capital you have raised, whether you are pre-product, whether your product is in market and generating revenue or has enough traction to show it's a viable business model, and whether you would be able to continue to grow without the resources from an accelerator. For us, we saw the value of tapping into the accelerators' LP network as potential customers and there was enough value there for us to negotiate some equity in exchange for the investment and connections.

Accelerators can also help court other investors. One major role of accelerators, if they are keeping their promise, is that they can help you raise additional funding and introduce you to other investors. Sometimes this works and sometimes it falls flat. I was introduced to Cultivation Capital via Engage, and the invested $3M in my Series A. Most accelerators require their founders to participate in demo day, as a mark that the cohort's time in the accelerator has ended and to provide an opportunity for startups to show what they are made of to other investors who are generally looking on with an interest to make an investment in one or more startups. Yet, not all accelerators are created equal when it comes to creating a space for follow-on investment. For example, YC founders can find themselves receiving follow-on investments with little to no diligence from investors who attend demo day. In essence, they are betting on YC's ability to court the best companies, and many investors will invest in every company that comes through a batch, although that might not be as common today with larger batch sizes, whereas other lesser-known accelerators might have relationships with investors to at least get you a call or meeting, but the heavy lift falls back on the founder. I believe founders can sometimes be led to believe that accelerators are a sure way to raise that next round of capital when in reality, that isn't the case for a lot of startups. Regardless, if you pick the right accelerator and look for the key things it can offer you then ideally by the time you "graduate" you will have the tools to raise your next round of funding. Also, when choosing an accelerator you should ask other founders about their experience and garner feedback when making a decision about which one to participate in.

9 Raising My Seed Round

There will be mountains you won't move.
Learn to climb.

—Unknown

By far my seed round was the hardest raise. What seed rounds look like today has drastically changed. For comparison, nine years ago Uber raised a $1.57 million seed funding round that valued the company at $3.86 million, and there were 32 investors in Uber's seed round with checks as small as $25,000. Today Crunchbase has dubbed large rounds of seed investments as "supergiant seed rounds," counting seed rounds that are larger than $5 million.

In 2017, I set out to raise $2 million in a seed round. It was no easy feat. My first mistake was believing that just because I had built an MVP, that we had customers and revenue, and that I was a second-time founder and CEO, things would be easier for me. Not only was I wrong, the process of raising a seed round would prove at times defeating. What I realized early on, or so I thought, was that I needed to be where the capital was, and for budding founders of tech startups that was the Bay area. So, I saw that Black Enterprise was holding their annual tech connect summit where Freada Kapor Klein was speaking. Freada is a well-known venture capitalist and, along with her husband, Mitch Kapor, is the founder of Kapor Capital. They are well known and respected in the Valley for not just their investing, but also their targeted investing in minority founders like myself. I decided that I was going to book a flight and purchase a ticket to attend the summit to meet her, so I did. I was sitting in the audience during her panel and realized that there wasn't going to be a break before the next speaker. As security rushed her off the stage, I snuck out the side door and quickly approached her as she was exiting. I told her that I had attended the conference with hopes of meeting her, and telling her about my startup, then named Exempt Me Now. She listened attentively and then gave me her card and proceeded to tell me to email her.

Goal accomplished! I not only made contact with one of my ideal investors, but she had given me her card. I went on to attend what was a really great conference.

Ultimately, I didn't get funded by Kapor. It was actually a really awkward experience overall, as during my first investor call the partner was walking and put me on hold to make a lunch order. It didn't take me long to realize that the call wasn't going anywhere. Founders will tell you there have been many meetings or initial calls that panned out this way, where they encountered a less than ideal situation that might have left them floored. You'd better learn to take the good with the bad, because there will be a lot of bad along the way. To be fair, although my experience was less than ideal, Kapor is known for investing in minority, Black, and Latinx founders and some close friends of mine. Tough break for me.

Nonetheless, the conference hadn't been a total bust. I ended up meeting other entrepreneurs, one of whom would become a good friend and would later help me launch my first entrepreneur-focused podcast, *From Solid Ground to Resilient*, via his media company and podcast network. I know you were probably thinking that the story was going to lead to me getting an investment, but it didn't.

I continued to raise capital for my seed round for months afterward. People actually didn't care about the traction or the product, and because I didn't have deep connections in the Bay area, it was actually very difficult for me to access investors.

As a minority founder raising capital you can get jaded very quickly; as a Black female founder, add several other layers to that. I've now done a good bit of angel investing myself in early-stage startups, and more than anything my experiences raising early funding (good and bad) have taught me what type of investor I don't want to be. I made a promise that I wouldn't ghost a founder after engaging with them or requesting diligence, and that I'd have the same respect for them as I desired for myself when I went out to raise funding.

What I have found is that receiving a "no" isn't the hardest part of rejection; it's the way you are treated in the process. So, what was the moment that turned things around for me? I mentioned in an earlier chapter that I participated in a pitch competition for New Orleans Entrepreneur Week. What I didn't mention is that the pitch competition was sponsored by Jim Coulter, one of the founders of TPG Capital. One perk each founder received for being invited to pitch during the competition was prep and call time with partners and associates from TPG Capital. During one of my prep calls, a partner at TPG Capital named Tim Millikin was listening in on the call. After I went on to lose the pitch competition, the following Monday I reached out to everyone on that call thanking them for their time. And though I had not been victorious, I was appreciative of the time they had taken with me to provide invaluable feedback. Tim responded to the email saying he felt I had a great startup and told me to reach out whenever I was in San Francisco, where he was based. About two months passed, with me continuing to reach out to investors and not having much luck. Then I decided that I was going to go out to San Francisco and schedule a few meetings with investors. I remembered that Tim had told me to reach out to him as well, so I did. Not only did he respond, he offered to meet over lunch so that I could catch him up on the business and talk more. As we sat for lunch, I brought him up to speed on my fundraising journey and admitted it had been tough. I couldn't quite land that lead or anchor investor that would bring on other investors. He began telling me about his company's area of focus, which was mostly later-stage companies, but that he personally invested in a few startups a year. He also shared that he could possibly help me connect with other investors and potential customers. I left that meeting not only with a commitment from Tim to help, but also a commitment from him to invest. He probably doesn't know this to this day, but his commitment was the fuel for an otherwise depleted tank of gas that renewed my spirits and gave me the energy I needed to continue my capital raise. I was able to use Tim's highly credible name with other investors, and because everyone will tell you, including investors themselves, that investors are followers, it also further legitimized the opportunity around the startup I was building.

Tim was the only investor I would find in the Bay. From there I began to garner attention and traction with other investors from the East and Southeast: the JumpFund, a collective investing in companies with at least one female founder; NextWave, which followed a similar thesis; a handful of angel investors like Tim; and a bit later, Mucker Capital, which would go on to co-lead my Series A.

When asked what I would recommend to founders looking to raise a seed round, there are a few things to consider:

1. Does your startup have traction? This isn't always necessary depending on your relationships, but it is important more often than not.
2. Have you built a team or shown the ability that you are a capable leader who can build a team?
3. Are you connecting with the right investors?
4. Have you created a contingency plan if it takes months to raise capital?

During our seed round we also agreed to convert our LLC to a Delaware corporation, which has been standard in the tech space for some time. We also for the first time created a small board. The importance of who sits on your board is directly connected to the investors you take on. This is why it's so important that you pick the right investors, and not be tempted to take on money from just anyone. For every investor you take on, you are giving up a stake in your company. You'll need investors who not only believe in you now but believe in you when the going gets tough.

10 Product Market Fit

The first phase has been written about extensively, and that is the search for product market fit. That phase is followed by a second phase, which in SaaS we call the search for repeatable, scalable, and predictable and profitable sales growth machines. Once you've got that predictable growth machine, you should hit the gas and just scale the business because you know that it's predictable and profitable and it just works. I think this is the most interesting part.

Sales: Remember Predictable, Repeatable Revenue?

Remember that the holy grail for many businesses is predictable, repeatable, and scalable revenue. This isn't just a startup thing but also how I found success with SGI. You want to develop a system where you can say, for example, that if you had one more salesperson they can perform X activity that will yield Y results. Creating a process where we can better forecast our cash flow and invest in our business to grow is one we continue to iterate on today. If you don't have a robust process, you have no idea how much new business a salesperson can bring in or how long it will take them to do it. So how much can you afford to pay? How many salespeople can you add? How can you grow?

There are three keys to repeatable revenue: first; predictable lead generation: second; identifying the companies you want to target, third; building your list, and tracking the conversions of your outreach campaigns from one step of your sales funnel to the next. You need to specialize one person for lead generation and qualification and another for demos and closing. Creating a consistent sales system can involve a lot of trial and error but it doesn't have to be completely random.

Document your entire process in a system so that every salesperson is following the exact same process and you get reliable numbers back.

For us, we prospected into cold accounts to generate new leads and business.

The next step is to identify your ideal customer profile build list. Then you build a list of contacts who match your profile email campaigns and you send out an email. You're asking someone to direct you to the right person about your offering; you're not selling anything, so you take the pressure off the interaction. Then you send a new email saying that so-and-so referred you; now it's not a cold email anymore. I'm a huge believer in finding some form of connection with enterprise-level customers.

Only sell the dream and the vision of the product for that particular customer. The next step is to have a live call where you sell the dream, get information about the prospect's goals, and help them connect their needs to your solutions. Once they see and believe the dream, the buy-in will be a lot easier. But you have to get them to buy in regardless of what stage the platform is. If you are like me and are the CEO of the company, then you are also a seller and are still on the front line, so some of the "sell" is also why the company you built is the right fit.

Your team will begin to create its own unique sales system through an iterative process. You will test different approaches, different emails and call scripts, refine them, and figure out what works best for your business. Our email open rate had dropped, and we started introducing video to one of the follow-up emails; our open rate significantly increased. We used a simple application called Bonjoro to make fun, down-to-earth videos.

The best signs that you're getting there is that you are growing Annual Recurring Revenue (AAR) quarter over quarter. It's not easy but it's possible.

At the end of 2020 we hired our first VP of Revenue to scale our sales operations and really put in the fundamental foundational elements needed to do this.

Customer experience and engagement are very important. We rely heavily on our customer success to give a stellar onboarding experience, and on product and user experience and interface design to give a great experience within the platform.

After all, we want to retain the customer and we want to grow revenue from that customer. You can create fancy, complicated Excel sheets and charts, but I would simplify them early on as much as possible. You can look at a funnel and it's very simple because the math represents only two key variables—what you put into the top of the funnel and what you convert.

So if you have 100 people in the top and you get 1 out, your conversion rate is 1% on that funnel. This is why lead generation is so important. Another variable that is also important is your average deal size because it determines the amount of monetization you're getting per customer. For us, my thought is how we can make this bigger over time. If our average contract value for our product is $35,000 or $500, the next important thing to know is how much it costs to actually close a deal, and how long it takes to close a deal. If you are a startup this is critical, because you are constantly monitoring your cash flow and burn rate.

Often I see business owners go out and make a sales hire too early. The key is to not use just salespeople to drive leads; this is where marketing comes into play.

Marketing is not one size fits all and marketers are missing out on a big opportunity by focusing on mass campaigns instead of what is referred to as boiling the ocean. I've found you can get much better results by focusing on just 100 clients who can make a big difference to your business and connecting with them in highly personalized creative ways.

This approach is called contact marketing and it can have response rates of 100%, compared to typical ad campaigns that celebrate 0.1% engagement rates.

The biggest problem most businesses in the B2B space face is access to important people or, should I say, the right people. Let's say you want to sell your professional services. How will you stand out above the noise and get noticed by the VP of procurement?

I'll go back to Solid Ground for a second here. We were targeting via contact marketing and I took on the challenge of handling the 12 accounts that were considered impenetrable. For each one, we researched the individual we needed to get in front of; sometimes that was the CEO and sometimes not. We searched everything from their LinkedIn profiles to articles and other tidbits about what their favorite hobbies were and so on. For one key account we were reaching out to, we sent the person responsible for awarding contracts a book signed by one of their favorite authors, who one of my advisors happened to know well. For another, we sent a personalized mug from their alma mater. This resulted in both contracts closing—not immediately, but ultimately.

Sometimes you have to get really creative to attract and build relationships with prospective customers. At the end of the day, there's an actual human doing the purchasing.

11 Raising a Series A

Get comfortable with the unknown.
Source: Lisa Warner Wardell

If, for the most part, you've proven you are the one to build this company, your insight and knowledge is deep enough that you might be able to transform the industry, you've proven that you can get others to back you (and stay with you), and your value proposition has been defended by customers who have used your product, then you might be ready to raise a Series A round of financing.

Series A rounds are generally geared toward early-stage, private companies. The size of the round can be very different. Similar to the drastic changes we've seen in seed round sizes, the same can be said for Series A round sizes, and they can range from 4 million to tens of millions of dollars. For many, this might also be the first institutional round of capital brought into your business. If you are enamored with the headlines, then you might think that the more money you raise the better, but this isn't the case. There are many factors you will want to take into consideration, one being your valuation and the other how much you need to get you to your next major milestone that will trigger your next round of funding. Before you approach a VC (or respond to one, if one has approached you), it's important to do your research. It's no secret that founders talk, but other investors talk too. I've asked founders as well as other VCs their thoughts on investors, and both have been very honest with me.

You also have to take into consideration whether you mesh well with your new prospective investors. Are they laid-back or formal? Do they enjoy the things you do? Or believe in similar causes that you do? What is a fit for one founder might not be a fit for you. Founders like us can sometimes feel like we have to take what's being offered to us, but I urge you to not fall down this rabbit hole, as it will only end up in disaster if you and the investor constantly clash—especially if they are a prominent investor on your cap table. When an investor decides they want to invest in your company they begin the courting process, but you have to think about whether you would want to work with them after the investment has been made.

I started raising a Series A round in the spring of 2019, but after a few conversations with investors quickly realized I wasn't going to get the valuation I wanted. So, I put my head down, decided to join Engage (one of the programs I spoke about previously), and began hiring the team I felt we needed to scale.

Then in late 2019, I knew it was time and started to meet with investors again. There was a lot we needed to do and we had only raised $2 million, which, for many reasons, proved to not be enough. So how do you know when your company is ready to raise a Series A? There really is no simple answer here. Most will say it's solely based on traction, but I know founders who have raised sizable Series A rounds with little to no traction. I know companies who have raised Series A rounds almost entirely off of hype. Founders who ask me this question want a definitive answer, or at least a few possible answers, to decide whether it's time. SaaS companies like ours tend to use metrics to make this decision. I also feel that investors are looking for how far you have come since you raised (if you have) a seed round.

We targeted an $8 million raise and began to seek introductions. This time we had better access to intro meetings and calls to investors via our seed investors. The accelerators we participated in came in handy when making introductions. Additionally, we decided that we were going to open up a second office in New York City.

Our opening up a second office in another city did not come as a surprise to my investors (thank goodness). They knew how committed I was to building the tech echo system in New Orleans, where I was from, but they also understood how difficult recruiting and raising subsequent rounds would be if I wasn't able to access the resources I needed. For me, a happy medium would be to continue to build our office in New Orleans, morphing it into a customer success office, while building out a second office in New York, where my R&D and sales team would sit. Note that this was pre-COVID-19, which created a world where teams now could work from anywhere.

Raising our Series A was a bit different than our seed round. I was a little better established as a tech founder than I was during my seed round, when literally no one knew me. I had investors that were not only willing to vouch for me but who for the majority were using their pro rata (see the Glossary if you don't know what this means). I understood what I needed to build out the company now more than ever. And I knew the team I needed to assemble if I were going to have any chance at being successful.

My Series A round was different, but what *wasn't* different was the due diligence we had to go through for investors looking to invest. However, this time we were better prepared; I mean really prepared. I feel preparation is one of the keys to raising a Series A. Simply put, as my grandmother used to say, your house needs to be in order. There's the initial commitment it takes to get your house in order and then there's the one to continue to make updates along the way until it's done.

Because I was prepared, I knew the majority of the questions that would be asked. I could turn materials around faster and usually answer questions on the spot. Nonetheless, diligence was still grueling. And now, after raising a small pre-seed round, a seed round, and a Series A round, I can say that it's different for us. It's harder. When I talked to my friends who were not women or Black, it became very clear to me that our diligence couldn't just be good enough or promising; it had to go above and beyond the call of duty. In some cases, I had to be able to answer the same questions in varying ways. There are a few lessons I learned about raising a Series A, and I share them here, in no particular order, as they are all important.

- **Look for key characteristics in your company.** You have a valid business model that can quickly be scaled and adapted according to the changing needs of your company, you have traction that shows a promising future, you're generating revenue at the scale you would like to see it, and the only way to grow faster and capture a larger market share is to raise capital. Though perhaps not perfect, you have found some product market fit with a product that customers have been using.
- **Gauging the right time to raise.** I wouldn't have guessed that I would be closing a Series A during COVID-19, but that's how life works. At any other given time, the timing really does matter. When I was raising my seed round, I started in late October. Big mistake—with the holidays approaching, you definitely don't want to start raising a round unless it's a given and you have located your investors or they have located you.
- **Your company story has to only get better.** I emphasized the importance of your narrative earlier, but it doesn't become less important. Now it's important to tie in your story with actual receipts and how your customers are using your product, how your team has grown, and how the mission has become even clearer since, say, the last time you raised capital.
- **Make sure your pitch is solid.** By now, you should have refined your pitch to where you could give it in your sleep. This is one area where I felt I really excelled. It was very clear

to the investors in the room that I knew our space and was an expert in the sector.

- **Deal room.** Probably the most important part of raising capital in your Series A is compiling a solid deal room that includes your financials, key performance indicators, legal docs, and other documents needed to back up the pitch you just gave.
- **Finding the right lead investor** and accompanying investors is very important; after all, your lead investor is about to join your board.
- **Getting the right deal terms really does matter.** Everything from investor rights to the valuation of your company matters, and not all investors will be founder friendly, so you'll need to work with legal counsel to ensure that you get the best deal.
- **Don't drag out the process.** You will want to run a tight fundraising campaign. Ensuring that your deal room and pitch are solid will make it easier to do this. Yet, there is still no magic trick; it all depends on your product and a number of other factors. It can all have an impact on how long your process is, but you don't want to make it that much harder because you're scattered.

As you raise your Series A round, you will also be expanding your board of directors. We started this book discussing the differences between a bootstrapped company and a venture-backed one. One key difference is that if you raise capital, you as the CEO and the company are not subjected to external supervision. The board, of whom most are investors, has an ownership interest in the company. This can cause a lot of anxiety for first-time founders because well, like me, they are not used to the added layer of board management. The main functioning role of a board is to help guide the company through big decisions, which include everything from hiring and firing to determining stock options and approving budgets. If you are trying to decide who should be on your board, note that some of this will be determined for you because whoever leads your Series A and Series B rounds will most likely join your board. I started off with three board members and now, post-Series A, I have a five-seat board.

We hold our board meetings once a quarter and between board meetings I have one-on-ones with board members on various topics. For example, Will Hsu, one of my board members and a managing partner at Mucker Capital, has spent a considerable amount of time outside of board meetings helping us with product and go-to-market strategy. Kristina Montague, a partner with the JumpFund, has spent time advising on customer verticals and ideal customer profiles.

As the CEO, it's your responsibility to set the agenda and run the board meeting, which for us usually lasts around three hours.

As you can imagine, the more money you raise, the higher the stakes continue to get. With each round of funding you take on dilution to the company as well as add additional stakeholders to the company. This is why it's imperative that you get your investors right because they will have a controlling stake in your company as you build it. This was a huge adjustment for me, coming from building my first company without investors or a board, as I didn't have to take time to prepare for board meetings or requests from board members throughout the year.

Finally, you want to make sure that you maintain a healthy relationship with your investors. I'll say this again: it's not their job, nor should they be attempting, to run your business. They are there to help grow the business and provide expertise and help with decision-making along the way.

12

Holy Crap—
A Pandemic!

*Come celebrate with me that every day something has
tried to kill me and has failed.*

—*Lucille Clifton*

Ever close a funding round during a pandemic? I don't think
many have. Yet, after all that due diligence and all those
meetings and calls, we finally got our round closed on March 22.

I remember weeks earlier, I could feel the tensions rising
across the country, particularly among VCs. Then SXSW, one of
the largest interactive conference and festivals drawing people
from film, music, interactive media, and tech from all across the
world, was canceled. I had planned to attend this year because
I was selected for the advisory council. I believe that SXSW
being canceled confirmed that COVID-19 would hit the tech
industry—and every industry, really—in an indisputable way.

People began to panic and though we were watching as the
entire world shut down around us, the United States had in
many ways been in a bubble.

To think, just weeks before we had Mardi Gras in New
Orleans. There was no talk about COVID-19 other than what
was happening in Wuhan, the original epicenter of the disease,
and we certainly had no idea that we would be impacted by it
in such a catastrophic way.

I sent my then COO and CTO a message telling them that
I felt we were going to be asked to quarantine. I told them

I had heard rumblings that the cities were going to start closing down. They felt I was slightly overstating what was to come, but the large majority of what I saw coming would end up coming to pass.

March 16th was my birthday. We had just celebrated with a meal at one of my favorite restaurants, Jack Rose, a few days prior. To this day my friends say I called it. I told them that my birthday dinner would be our last dinner together. The next day Mayor Latoya Cantrell ordered all restaurants to close; schools and other establishments would follow suit.

Our office in Bryant Park, which we had just moved into January 1st, would do the same.

Here we were, living in a real-life pandemic. My mentors said they had never experienced anything like this, but no one had. The only other time that my normalcy had completely changed overnight was after Hurricane Katrina. That wasn't a pandemic but it was a national humanitarian crisis, one that left me and my college friends unsure of what was going to happen next and in a state of utter shock.

I come from a family of healthcare professionals. My sister is a nurse practitioner; so is? my best friend and my close cousin. They would be called to duty in a way that would make us fear for their health and safety. Like thousands and thousands across the United States and millions around the world, these first responders, front-liners, would become the unsung heroes of the pandemic.

For tech? First came the broken term sheets. Yes, investors were backing out of their commitments. They were turning away from the founders they had shaken hands with, spent hours in diligence with, and promised to journey with them to scale.

Then came the theories that investing would slow down altogether. I mean, the *New York Times* even reported that "the great unwinding" of the tech boom had started. Even with all the capital that had been raised in venture, many felt that investing would potentially dry up.

The pandemic certainly had an impact on the tech industry as those not already doing so moved to a new normal of working from home. Some VCs paused investing, and some tech companies like Airbnb began laying off large percentages of their staff in an effort to weather the pandemic, while other industries not related to hospitality or events accelerated growth. This was certainly the case with Resilia. We were in an unique position. We had just closed on a round of funding and unlike ever before philanthropy was in unprecedented times. The real winners, however, were companies like Amazon, Zoom, and grocery delivery apps like Instacart, which benefited from millions of people staying at home.

For small businesses, a report by McKinsey revealed that it could take five years for the overall sector to recover to pre-crisis GDP levels. If a small business doesn't recover at least by 60% within a year's time, the chances it will survive at all are very small. When operating in crisis mode, you feel the pressure to fix everything that's wrong with your business. The problem is that you stretch yourself too thin and as a result you fail to move the needle anywhere; instead, focus on your weakest link, starting with the most fundamental layer of your business.

Similar to Maslow's hierarchy of needs, businesses also have a five-layer pyramid of needs that you must tend to, from the foundation upward. At the base of the pyramid is sales money coming in. Above sales sits profit, which gives you stability and allows you to scale. Then comes order, which means that you have effective business systems that create staff autonomy. Next comes impact, which enables you to shift business and actions from transactions to transformative experiences, which I find to be of the most importance for businesses that are able to move quickly.

PPP loans and other grants would come slowly, if, for many, at all. I watched as some of my friends in the hospitality sector had to lay off their entire staff to stay open while other of my friends with online marketing and product companies thrived, as people used the extra time that being locked indoors provided them to pick up a different skill or take an online course.

No doubt, even as you read this we are still facing the real-life challenges of COVID-19.

The impact of COVID-19 on startups would be seen in some unexpected ways. It taught me and reminded me of a few things:

Be of service.

Cash remains king.

We are all resilient.

Get comfortable with the unknown.

Source: Lisa Warner Wardell

Prioritizing Mental Well-Being

2020 reminded me that it's a luxury to be able to prioritize mental health even when it shouldn't be, and to have the ability to be able to say no constantly far more than saying yes. There will never be enough meditation and mindfulness that will ease the mind of a person struggling to make ends meet. For my family and friends in the healthcare sector, saying "no" during COVID-19 to certain behavior that put their own lives at risk as healthcare providers also proved to be difficult. This is why it is important to acknowledge that being able to prioritize mental health is a luxury that not everyone can afford.

When you are in business you really need to get into the habit of asking what the highest and best use of your time is and say no to virtually everything else. Mental and physical health counts here too, and we'll talk more about that later. Luxury or not, I believe it is safe to say that you can't do your best work if you're not taking care of yourself, mentally and physically.

It's key that you make time for yourself to think deeply about the most important aspects of your business. I was in a chat with a few founders and someone mentioned feeling guilty when they would rest. This is super common and I'd say it's in the DNA of founders and lots of others as well. In other words, folks feel guilty for resting so they might even substitute time of rest with other projects or forms of work. Try reading a book, or catching up on industry news that you find interesting, or going for a walk.

With being home during a pandemic, my workload actually increased, and the number of Zoom calls that were on my daily schedule was beyond insanity. It's tough to really spend time on the right strategy or unify existential threats to your business if you're scheduled constantly or if you feel like you can't find time for your mind to rest. This is just part of the focus; you need to make time for the hard problems and the key areas where you can add the most value to the business, such as making key hiring decisions, putting the right organizational structures in place, and building a growth environment for your team. This has been very difficult for me as well, but nine months into the pandemic, on a Friday, I had 10 back-to-back Zoom calls. That was my breaking point, where I knew I would not be able to function to my best ability if I continued this.

So to summarize the key takeaways on this topic, say no more often and practice it. When you learn to say no, it will become clear which things you really need to say yes to as your company grows and you learn to trust your team to take on things. You have to focus on where you can have the most impact and let your team take on the other things. Are you invited to a lot of speaking engagements? If the event doesn't accomplish a key goal for you, could it be great exposure for somebody else? If yes, invite someone to go in your place. This goes back to having a support staff who can help protect your time and remove the day-to-day distractions that keep you from focusing. You'll have your seasons of "yes" but the more you can do now will equate to the more you can do for others later.

It may seem like you'll have more time someday, when your company is larger and more established and has more employees, but you're wrong, because time still remains your most valuable asset. It can be hard to block time out and tune out the noise, but I've learned, especially during 2020's pandemic, social unrest, record-breaking hurricanes, and election. This is why, more than anything, in 2020 we encouraged employees to take time off when they needed it for their health and well-being. It's equally important for you as a leader to do the same.

13 The Murder of George Floyd, Breonna Taylor, and BLM

We have taken the baton.

—Opal Tometi

They say that we become desensitized after a while. I don't know if that's true.

A few weeks before George Floyd was murdered, I remember talking to a senior writer at *Essence* magazine. I had just announced our Series A raise and we were doing an interview. I remember telling her that because of COVID-19 and everything that was happening I didn't feel excited about the raise. I'm an empath. I feel the pain of others deeply. I'm not happy when others aren't winning. I was reading emails in my founder groups from founders who had to lay off their entire staff, shutting their doors. She softly reminded me that it was still important to find joy in wins. I took heed of that advice, not knowing that just a few weeks later we would witness the murder of a 46-year-old Black man in Minneapolis. What we saw next would become our generation's version of a civil rights movement, an era I believe that the history books will describe as the Black Lives Matter movement.

When you are running a company and you have not one but two historic events that happen in a short period of time, something neither you nor anyone else has ever experienced, you rack your brain on what to do next.

I've found that when you don't know how to show up, you always show up as yourself.

The events that would play out in the aftermath of the murders of George Floyd and Breonna Taylor, who the world would also find out about, would be unlike any other I'd come to witness.

Note, during college I bore witness to and was involved with marches following Jena Six. In August 2006, a Black student in Jena, Louisiana, asked if he could sit under a tree on campus or if it was reserved for whites. Three nooses hung from the tree the next day. In December, six Black boys beat a white student, and five suspects were charged with attempted murder. Civil rights leaders across the nation, college groups like those that formed on my campus, would protest the charges.

Almost 16 years later, I would be close to another incident that would cause mass protests across the nation. The murder of Alton Sterling, who was unarmed, selling CDs in Baton Rouge, the city of my alma mater and where I was living at the time of his death, sent shock waves across the country.

Though we are not new to social injustices being committed against Black people, this time the pain and outcry for George Floyd would be heard all across the world. CNN showed a map of the United States; every single state reported mass protests. In London, people filled the streets to protest police brutality. Pain and anger filled the voices of those who spoke across the news channels, there were tears from the most unexpected sympathies, and individuals of every race, creed, and background would move to the streets.

Because of COVID-19, I had retreated back to New Orleans and had been sheltering at home. I belong to many groups, but the email of one in particular caught my attention. I'm a part of a small-business group, based in New Orleans, of very successful CEOs of companies that range in size upward of $1 billion valuations.

My white colleagues were trying to determine how they could help, and ways they could be anti-racist.

One colleague emailed that his team said that using the term POC is often used to avoid having to address Black people, and our very painful history in the United States, head-on. It's not enough to be anti-racist, you also have to practice "anti-Blackness," which is the root of a lot of oppression and racism in the United States. Even for non-Black people with dark skin, such as Filipinos and Indians, some of the racism they experience is no doubt rooted in anti-Blackness.

I responded to his email with full transparency:

June 3, 2020, 1:16 p.m.

Yes, "people of color" can dilute the message and has been used to erase Black people from positions of leadership, funding, and opportunity. I am happy someone on your team called this out and that you were able to receive it. As far as immediate and longer-term change, some of you have mentioned ways, but:

Ask yourself, yesterday was Give Nola Day. Did I use that opportunity to give back to a Black-led nonprofit in my community?

Ask yourself, I'm an LP/investor; have I ever invested in a Black-led company?

Ask yourself, I'm a leader of an organization/company over 10+ people; do I have Black people in leadership positions?

Ask yourself, I'm a leader of an organization/company of over 50 people; does the makeup (%) of my organization look like the makeup of New Orleans?

I resisted sending this because Black people are tired and exhausted. I've been tired and exhausted from battling racism since I was 8 years old when my classmate called me the N word and my teacher condoned it. I've been tired and exhausted since I was 15 years old when cops drew guns on us at a Wendy's (we were just band students gathering after a game, not the group of thugs they called us). My best friend, our drum major, just happened to work at City Hall in a student work position then. She went to the basement and read the report on their justification for drawing guns on us, the lies they had told about us. Or when my friend and his best friend were 17, driving to prom with their dates, a police car behind them pulled them over and, laughing, made them lay on the ground face down in front of their dates and in their tuxedos. They ended up getting a ticket for littering because my brother's friend flicked a toothpick out of the back window at a stop. My brother's now a Chief Master Sergeant in the Air Force. I've been tired and exhausted since I was a student at LSU, where we were greeted with the most absurd racism I'd witnessed to date. Ironically, you can probably now find my face plastered on every LSU campaign as one of their favorite faces of diversity. I've been tired and exhausted since my 20s as I started my first business, and now in my 30s as a black tech founder. Thanks, by the way, for all the congratulatory messages about my funding round, it was hard to respond because I myself felt no joy. The fundraising journey isn't just hard and exhausting for Black founders. It too is riddled with racism, as I recall that time (that time being six months ago) when a partner fell asleep in the conference room two minutes into my presentation with him and another partner from a large, well-known fund.

My white neighbor asked if I was going to the protest yesterday, to which I responded no not today, but they should. Though I've given in many ways, I've protested in my teens and all of my college career, I protested in my 20s, and what I've realized now in my 30s is that my entire life, every single day, I am protesting and fighting. And I am tired.

Though I do not condone violence, rioting, or looting, you have to ask yourself, if Sevetri's experience has been the above . . . a college educated, community/business leader, what have the experiences of other Black people been like? Maybe that can help you better understand why cities are burning, and how you are connected to the problem as much as the solution.

No need for a response, just thanks for stepping up.

The Talk I Had With My Team

Ahead of that email, I also shared a personal message to my team on our All Hands the Monday after George Floyd's death, which was very different from the virtual Zoom conversation I had with my team.

What I told them was this:

I grew up going to predominantly white schools. There I faced significant racism. I recalled going through my elementary and middle school years, and asking my Mama why she kept sending us to schools with kids who were like this. Kids who called us names and clearly treated us so differently. She would respond to me, "You belong there, too." So when I went to LSU I was shocked to see that some of the same racism and discrimination was still alive and well. I realized that education also had nothing to do with racism and social injustice. There in college I learned how systemic racism and overt racism still prevailed. I wasn't just in Louisiana for Alton Sterling and Jena Six, I was there for Hurricane Katrina. COVID-19 was the first time many had experienced their entire worlds shifting overnight. For me that experience was Katrina. The aftermath of Katrina revealed the divide in America's thinking on race and racism. I feel that the racial divide on our college campus intensified, especially as evacuees sheltered in LSU's stadium and displaced students from neighboring colleges, including HBCUs, enrolled. I recall students from other campuses criticizing us, asking the question "Why go there if you aren't treated well?" The thing that I most recalled was what my mother had told me as a kid in elementary school: "You belong here, too."

You may ask why am I speaking to social injustice and racism in this book. To that I would respond that if the events surrounding George Floyd, Breonna Taylor, and the countless other victims of police brutality and other injustices didn't warrant conversations within your company, then you ignored them. They not only did exist but they still do and will continue to play a significant role in how employees across the country and world look at their employer and company culture.

The social justice awakening or reckoning that happened in 2020 also propelled people to begin to "buy Black." I spoke to why buying Black has to go beyond consumer buying.

What was largely missing from the race conversation was calling upon corporations, large-scale charities, and government organizations to also buy Black. After all, the U.S. government is the largest buyer in the world, spending an estimated $500 billion on contracts annually, and that number will rise due to the global COVID-19 pandemic. Thus, you would be hard-pressed to find a Black-owned tech company like mine (Resilia) on these lists. While individual consumers can and should do their part, moving the needle requires entities with deep and wide reach to adopt this mandate as well. To this point, buying Black means increasing the number of contracts and procurement opportunities for Black-owned companies—many of which exist to help change systems (think infrastructure and technology) by offering innovative solutions to age-old problems. In other words, companies that are helping transform the way we do business as usual.

As a software company that sells directly to cities, private foundations, public charities, and corporations (we also categorize them as those that deploy capital to programs, initiatives, and organizations), I am acutely aware that those who stand to gain from this increased velocity in new funding are white men– or white women–led software companies. Black people in these corporate ranks are practically nonexistent. According to a report from the Center for Talent Innovation, a nonprofit group sponsored by large companies (including Morgan Stanley, Pfizer, and Disney), only four companies in the Fortune 500—Merck & Co., TIAA, Tapestry, and Lowe's—now have a Black chief executive. This is down from seven less than a decade prior.

The Role of Philanthropy in Creating Equity

Because of its purchasing power, philanthropy also has the ability to do business with Black vendors, consultants, and software providers. We've seen people of color elevated to positions of power in order to lead organizations with multibillion-dollar endowments—such as Darren Walker with the Ford Foundation and La June Montgomery Tabron with the W.K. Kellogg Foundation—who have not been shy about calling out racial disparity and injustice before now.

Yet even heads of larger, philanthropic organizations still find themselves in difficult situations, tasked with proving their value and leaving little room to create equitable practices as they report into boards and other stakeholders who may have not adopted these practices. As Angela Williams, CEO of Easterseals, once said in *The Chronicle of Philanthropy*, a popular philanthropy outlet: "You can't really afford mistakes because they're not necessarily forgiven. It's about dotting i's, crossing t's, and spending the extra time to prove that you deserve the position that you hold."

During a time like this—when money is flowing and a new fund is announced every day because of COVID-19 and social injustice—technology plays a necessary role in leveling the playing field and ensuring that equity exists for organizations of all shapes, colors, and sizes. Thus, companies and organizations that are in positions to invest in technology and innovation should also ask: Are we doing our best to also support non-consumer-facing (B2B) Black-owned businesses? In other words, it's incumbent upon decision-makers to look beyond the myth that technology solutions built by Black-founded companies simply don't exist, and to likewise develop mechanisms to seek out these "hidden figures."

Systemic Issues Facing Black-Led Technology Companies

While it is certainly true that Black technology founders exist, it's also true that Black founders face barriers to funding, and it's been this way for decades. Once they do receive the funding, Black-led startups face similar barriers when they set out to sell to enterprise-level customers.

As a Black female founder in enterprise software (who has now raised over $10 million in capital), I make up a very small demographic within our space. Though my fundraising journey has not been an easy one, I took note of the vast similarities between my experience fundraising and my experience selling enterprise software.

During my fundraising, I had a candid conversation with a well-known female VC; we discussed how white male founders not only have the benefit of their network in raising capital, but also the benefit of their network when it comes to who buys their product. The "good ol' boys club" is just as pervasive in funding as it is during the sales process and securing contracts. White founders—by way of their professional or investor networks—are introduced from one colleague to the next, and this often gives them an extreme advantage.

These highly influential networks decide which technologies get adopted, and are often referred to as "kingmakers." In the current landscape, having a product that stands out from the competitive set simply isn't going to be enough. Adoption is a critical component when you are seeking to scale. Because of the networks and circles white-led companies are in, they are able to get their software products adopted at a higher velocity. Additionally, by leveraging a company's resources and thus reach, these startups are catapulted to scale much faster.

Think about it this way: When Peter Thiel or Jeff Bezos invests in your company, you don't just get their monetary investment, you also gain access to their network—and this is where the backdoor deals happen. In other words, if you aren't a part of this network, you never have the opportunity to compete. Where there is no real opportunity to compete, there is no real equity. In many ways, this is the workings of an invisible hand, but not the one we think about when we refer to Adam Smith's *The Wealth of Nations.*

When I think about kingmakers of the Black-led tech community who can champion our products, few (if any) come to mind.

If allies want to break the barriers of success within tech and other areas of contracting, they can start by taking a comprehensive look at their vendor list and with whom they choose to do business. This call to action isn't only for white decision-makers but also for Black, Indigenous, and People of Color who sit in positions of power—whether on a board seat or wielding the signature pen that can sign off on a contract opportunity.

The following is a handful of suggestions for any organization with purchasing power (corporations, private foundations, cities) that wants to build equity in the process of choosing vendors and contractors.

- **Audit your vendors:** If allies really want to break down silos and ensure that equitable practices are being instituted, I implore you to take an audit of who you do business with, and award contract and partnership opportunities to qualified Black-owned companies.

- **Access to procurement and supplier opportunities:**
  Increase participation in contracting and supplier opportunities. Companies and organizations have to define, but
  also choose, the vendors they use. Generally, this is done
  through supplier discovery, which leads to a shortlist, and
  then onto an advanced supplier review in some cases. In
  other cases, the company or organization can elect to purchase software, hardware, or any other product or service
  through a single- or sole-source agreement.

- **Alter organizational and corporate governance:**
  Recently, Reddit co-founder Alexis Ohanian resigned
  from his company's board and asked to be replaced by a
  Black candidate. Several days later Reddit named Y Combinator CEO Michael Seibel as his replacement. Let's go
  a step further: It's not only important to add Black faces
  to boards, it's also important that they are encouraged
  and allowed to help create equitable practices for minor-
  ities and Black people within the company infrastructure.
  Otherwise, their placement on the board only does just
  that—fill a vacant seat.

14 My Hopes, and Losing an Icon

On some days things will go exactly how you planned them, on other days you'll have to be resilient.
—Sevetri Wilson

The death of Chadwick Boseman, who starred as Black Panther in the record-breaking Marvel movie about a utopian world named Wakanda, had an immense impact on me.

Maybe it was because by the time we heard of his passing so much had happened. Maybe it's because of the faces of millions of children who were giddy about having a superhero who looked like them. It was likely a mix of all of these things.

Regardless of the exact reason, it made me recenter on my own internal "why." What legacy am I leaving and how can I solidify this within the span of my life, however long that will be? How can I not just be successful in terms of building a company where not only team benefits from it, but that from its success hundreds of other opportunities for others emerge? What was so powerful about Chadwick Boseman was that a young Black kid from South Carolina accomplished his wildest dreams. His life is a reminder that each of us can do the same.

The Role Technology Plays

I think to what we are building at Resilia; it's time to shift our collective thinking about what it means to be a society that provides equal opportunity, and technology has a role in this. For every headline we read about an instance of police brutality, we read 10 more about the gross inequities at every major institution in the United States. Wall Street? Naturally. Hollywood? Check. Mainstream media? You bet. Higher education? Sad, but true.

But the nonprofit sector—which has taken on greater responsibility in our cities, particularly when it comes to providing services for historically marginalized communities—should be immune to gender and racial discrimination, shouldn't it? Surely cities and other grantors offer equality of opportunity as they distribute resources, considering the vital role nonprofits play in addressing the systemic factors that lead to inequality.

In fact, there are significant disparities in funding for nonprofits led by people of color. According to a 2020 study published by The Bridgespan Group and Echoing Green, (BGEG) led nonprofits receive an average of 24% lower revenue and have access to 76% less unrestricted net assets. Not only do Black indigenous and People of Color led nonprofits have fewer resources to work with in the first place, but they also can't access resources on an ongoing basis to address any crises or changing conditions that may arise.

Why does this matter? Because the environment in which you are raised, and the resources you can access, will have a profound impact on your future. As a Black female tech founder serving the nonprofit sector, I don't expect my experiences and outcomes to be exactly the same as my white male and female peers. I didn't expect when I started my company and raised venture capital that doors would just be open for me to walk through. I knew it was up to me. What I shouldn't have to deal with is the need for back channels, a secret network of white, Ivy League-educated classmates, or twice as much proof of my capabilities in order to cross the threshold. Yet, the latter is the reality for most Black founders or leaders—in both the for-profit and nonprofit sectors, and others from underrepresented backgrounds as well, say if you grew up in a rural area.

Using the nonprofit sector as a proxy (and it's a fair one, as the sector accounts for 5.6% of U.S. GDP and more than 12% of the workforce), it's a good time to step back and look at the role technology plays in crossing these divides. At a time when nonprofits are working to address major issues like COVID-19 and racial injustice, technology is necessary for leveling the playing field and ensuring that equity exists for organizations of all shapes, colors, and sizes.

Grantors that are preparing to deploy capital should ask themselves this question: Are we doing our best to create an equitable capital allocation process? It's important to look for technology solutions that can alleviate barriers to entry for nonprofits, but education is a crucial part of this process. For example, organizations often think (incorrectly) they lack access to the resources that can help them track and report outcomes. A recent report conducted by BDO and *The Nonprofit Times* found that the top three reporting challenges cited by nonprofits are a lack of a consistent framework for collecting and sharing data, a lack of human resources, and the inability to gather information on the impact of programs.

This is why part of the mandate for grantors should be to identify these types of nonprofits (often led by community organizers from underrepresented groups or People of Color) and equip them with the right technology so they can begin to track important benchmarks. Will this take extra effort on behalf of the grantor? Yes. But holding a nonprofit accountable for outcomes, much like you would a for-profit company, is the first step in generating lasting impact.

The goal of any program is to secure positive outcomes and sometimes neutralize or alleviate the undesirable ones, but without accurate data, these outcomes are impossible to track. Since evidence of effectiveness is required for obtaining grants and funding, this must be the primary focus for nonprofits. Digital tools will allow them to rigorously track and report outcomes, communicate with grantors, and ultimately secure funding. The collection of concrete data is a way to eliminate bias in the distribution of resources. When grantors can see objective measures that demonstrate an organization's effectiveness, they will be more inclined to support it. Full stop.

Digital platforms can offer transparency on both sides, engender trust, and build connective tissue within what often feels like a hierarchical and systematically biased system. While technology can't solve every problem, its existence alone is proof of progress. When we choose to use it for the greater good—in this case, to help update worn-out systems that don't provide equity in the process of securing nonprofit funding, which leads to worse outcomes for organizations and communities alike—we can at least know we're moving in the right direction. Perhaps this will lead to a future in which Black, Indigenous, and POC-led nonprofits have taken enough steps to finally walk through the door.

On Building Generational Wealth

As an entrepreneur, creator, builder, thinker, and human, you will evolve over time and sometimes you have to make a shift to do it. Sometimes what you thought was going to be your path might turn out completely differently.

I was born and raised in a small town in Louisiana. I was a first-generation college student. My father didn't attend college, and my mother didn't finish. Yet, they pushed education on me. If I had to go back and tell myself something when I was just starting a business, it would be what I now tell you: You have so many options and so many ways to be successful. What works for one may not work for you. You have to figure out what works for you. You have to put people around you, mentors, the right friends, peers who will build you up and not tear you down, champion you! You will make mistakes, a lot of mistakes, you will misjudge a situation a time or two, but don't look back. Some of us become stagnant and so we don't reach our full potential. But that's on us; no one is coming to save us. You have to design the life you want. My therapist told me once, you have had the experience of being poor, now God will give you the experience of being rich. Being rich doesn't have to mean material things such as money, but in this case this is exactly what he meant.

Building wealth is something that's important to me and is a direct correlation to how we build abundance in our community. No, I don't believe that creating more billionaires is the key to unlocking more doors. Yet I do believe that when people like myself have the ability to create wealth, we have a fundamental duty that's ingrained in us to not only give back but to change the course of others' lives with the resources we acquire. This is why it's so important that our businesses are set up for success and can create profitability so that we aren't always building at a deficit. You can build a million-dollar business, but if you can't turn a profit and keep some of this profit, or in a startup you can't create a liquidity event, or find other avenues to generate cash and assets, then it will be really difficult to generate wealth. I've taken a lot of risks as an entrepreneur that some might not find that they can stomach. I find that as a group entrepreneurs just tend to have a higher tolerance for risk taking than the general public. Early on in business, I put everything into my business. There was a time when I was paying my own team out of my own pocket so that I wouldn't miss a payroll. There is this belief that you always pay yourself first, but if you are running a business and you have hired people you are responsible for these individuals. For me more times than not it would prove to be worth the sacrifice.

As I was able to grow SGI for example, and turn a profit, I accumulated more cash. From here I was able to invest this cash into real estate (this could be buying your first home), other startups, businesses, and stocks. Remember if it weren't for SGI I wouldn't have started Resilia, and if weren't for my ability to invest my own capital to get it going it wouldn't exist today.

Additionally, your network begins to broaden. In business and in life you meet other people along the way, and they bring opportunities to you as well to invest in. Wealth accumulates over time, so there is no need to feel like you have to make gobs of money right now; contrary to social media, you aren't actually running out of time. A few other strategies can help you refine your business practices so that you can "get rich" in business:

- Pay people well: One thing I've always done is to pay my team members and contractors market value or better. I'm a negotiator and stay within my means, but I'll never low-ball someone in this regard. There have even been times when I knew a contractor was lowballing themselves that I increased the contract price so that they would understand their own value. The same goes for team members who were having difficulty negotiating their own salaries. You want to keep your best talent for as long as possible, so eventually lowballing people will catch up with you. I don't want to create opportunities just for myself, but I also want to help others do the same.

  Note: You don't have to be the CEO to build wealth. It's a process of saving money, reducing your expenses and lifestyle, and investing. I bought my first condo, now an investment property, when I was 23 years old while making a $50,000 salary.

- Collect Receivables in a timely fashion: One factor that impedes business owners from being able to turn a profit is that they don't collect money. This is less of an issue for consumer-driven businesses. Yet, failure to collect on invoices and slow-paying customers can literally kill a business. You can set some systems in place where you can monitor your average collection time, and work to drive this under 30 days.

- Investing: Though small business owners and entrepreneurs are mostly risk-takers, they can look at investing in other things as a high-risk. This is why it's important to sit down with a financial planner to truly understand what's available to you, and create an investment strategy.

- ■ Understanding taxes: As you grow, taxes can be overwhelming. Yet there are some advantages you have as a business and startup, whether that be tax credits or tax reduction (legally, of course)! You have to ensure that you are working with a Certified Public Accountant who has worked with someone like you. I've had to change CPAs over time because as my business grew, my needs grew as well. One way businesses fail is that they get caught up in a never-ending cycle of owing the Department of Revenue and IRS money—one thing we know is that they will always collect one way or another.

Hold yourself accountable to yourself. When I look back over the last 12 years of being an entrepreneur (I told you I'm no overnight success story), I have mostly fond memories, even during the deep lows when people wrote me off, I became stronger for it. So, to all the entrepreneurs out there looking to catch their first break or take their company to the next level, or get that first investor check: Keep going. Work smarter, believe more in yourself, know you are capable and competent. Don't stay down too long. Yes, it's going to be hard, really hard. You're going to feel like giving up, and even if you fail, don't drown in defeat.

Remember, when it's all said and done people will remember most how you lived your life, how you championed and stood up for people and yourself. Don't let this life break you.

For me? I'm stronger now, I've let grace settle in. I've counted my blessings more times than I've counted my failures, I've counted the people who counted me in and not the ones who counted me out. I show up daily, more resilient than ever.

Appendix

Glossary

Solid Ground's Rate Sheet

Resilia's Investor Deck

Online Resources

Glossary

Accelerator: A hub where startups are given mentorship, space to work on their ideas, and sometimes seed capital.

Accredited investor: Defined by the SEC (Securities and Exchange Commission) as "A natural person with income exceeding $200,000 in each of the two most recent years or joint income with spouse exceeding $300,000 for those years and a reasonable expectation of the same income level in the current year; or a natural person who has individual net worth, or joint net worth with the person's spouse, that exceeds $1 million at the time of the purchase, excluding the value of the primary residence of such person." In layman's terms, it is a rich individual potentially interested in investing in your company.

Acquisition: When one company or investment group buys another company.

B2B: Business-to-business, meaning you offer a product or service to other companies.

B2C: Business-to-consumer, meaning you offer your products or services to other consumers.

Bootstrapping: If you've heard it once, you've heard it at least twice. A lot of people will quote the Three Fs: friends, family, and fools. These channels are often where you get your first cash to get things going. If you are using very little capital and proving your hypothesis, you are successfully bootstrapping.

Bubble: A moment in an economic cycle where an industry or company does not realize that it might be overvalued and overinflated. When a tech bubble bursts, a lot of startups go bust and investors lose their money.

Burn rate: How fast you go through your cash. The majority of startups lose money before they break even and then make a profit.

Cash flow positive: When more money is coming in than going out. When you deduct your expenses from your earnings, you have a positive amount in your bank account. Staying in the black, especially when you are self-funded, is the name of the game!

Churn rate: The annual percentage rate at which customers stop subscribing to a service or employees leave a job.

Cliff: Usually applies to vesting schedules (shares given to employees over time). Cliffs can be a device for the CEO to fire employees or let them leave without giving them stock within a limited period of time (usually one year). There are horror stories from Silicon Valley about early employees being cut just before they get to receive their equity stake. Cliffs are also used on CEOs by investors to make sure the CEO sticks around after getting the cash.

Crowdfunding: The act of using a site like Kickstarter to get a tribe of early fans together to give you money to help you get your product/site launched. You keep 100% of your company and only give away a percentage of the total you raise to the crowdfunding portal.

Crowdsourcing: Getting information for free from people on the internet or using a survey.

Deck (aka pitch deck):   A presentation that covers all aspects of your business in a succinct and exciting way. If you ever need inspiration for a good deck, check out how Elon Musk uses his to demonstrate the TESLA Powerwall.

Demographic: A term that is frequently used in marketing to describe the age, gender, income, education, and occupation of your ideal customers.

Disruptive technology: Any tech that consumers to think differently about an industry and then adopt that technology as the new norm. Examples include Uber, Lyft, Airbnb, and JetSmarter.

Early adopters: The first users of your product. They will typically be key influencers and active on social media. They will give you your most honest and sometimes overly direct feedback. If you can identify these people effectively and have them interact with your startup from an early stage, you can get lots of free exposure.

Ecosystem: As with an ecosystem in nature, a startup eco-system has its food chain. There are the hunters, the herd, and the bottom feeders. Work out where you are and where you want to be, then get involved in your startup ecosystem. If the city you are in doesn't have incubators, accelerators, co-working spaces, mentors, and investors, you should (a) move to another city, or (b) start your own ecosystem.

Equity crowdfunding: Equity crowdfunding is just like reg-ular crowdfunding but instead of getting money in return for a fee, you pay a fee to the crowdfunding site and a percentage of the company to investors.

Evangelist: Someone inside your organization who is your number-one fan. They love your company so much that they often go above and beyond their expected role to help promote your company. If you find an evangelist, hire them.

Exit strategy: How you plan to sell your company to give you and your investors a return on their investment. This ranges depending on the industry, but a standard multiple with tech-nology investments seems to be 10x.

Freemium: A freemium approach is when you give your basic product away for free and then try to upsell other features to your customers. It is a common and proven technique to acquire more users.

Gamify: If you gamify something, you add a game layer to your product that encourages people to use it with rewards of various kinds. See Foursquare and how they used virtual badges and the "Mayor" badge to encourage people to use their app.

Growth Hacking: A term first used by Sean Ellis (Dropbox) to describe a marketing technique that focuses on quickly finding scalable growth through nontraditional and inexpensive tactics such as the use of social media. Other companies that have effectively used this technique are Airbnb and Foundr.

Intellectual Property (IP): Intellectual property covers patents, trademarks, and copyrights. It is a good way to protect your "secret sauce." Generally I think of them like this: Patents—the DNA of your product. They are typically used to protect your design. Trademarks—they are used to protect your brand and depending on which one you register, you can add a ™ or ® (registered trademark) next to your logo. Copyrights—they are used to protect your creative content (like film, music, or art) and allow you to use a © symbol on your content.

Iterate: To try something, refine it, try again, and keep trying, using small steps until successful.

Launch: When you start a company, website, or app. It is the euphoric moment when you feel that the blood, sweat, and tears were worth it. Companies can either have a soft launch (minimal press exposure and staying in beta) or celebrate with a launch party, which can be at major startup events like CES or a Startup Week.

Lean Startup: A startup that has been launched with as little startup capital as possible while getting data that can be used to improve the product. Speed is the key factor here.

LTV/CAC ratio (lifetime value/cost to acquire customer): This compares the lifetime value (LTV) of a customer to the cost to acquire them (CAC).

Market penetration: You will frequently hear the question, "How much of the pie are you trying to get?" from investors. What they mean is how much market share will be yours and in what time period?—in other words, what your market penetration will be.

Minimum viable product (MVP): The simplest form of your product. This can be used to attract beta users/early adopters or to pitch for funding.

Monetize: How you make money. Do you sell online, offer consulting services, or sell face to face? Without a way to monetize, most businesses die. The only exceptions are well-funded tech startups where a bet has been made that the site will get enough users so that a monetization strategy can eventually be executed. This is highly risky but the reward is high.

Pivot: A change in direction as a company. This is a key moment in the life of a startup and can make or break it. A well-known pivot is when Fab went from being a gay social network to being an e-commerce curator.

Responsive design: An integral part of a website that has been built to function well across all devices. Your site might appear completely differently on the web compared to mobile but as long as your end users are always considered, you will be fine.

ROI: Return on investment. When an investor puts money into a company, he wants to know what he will get out, the ROI. The investor(s) will also want to know how long it will take to get their ROI.

Runway: How long your cash will last and when you think it will run out. The key here is knowing when to start pitching for investment so you can time it to come in before you run out of cash.

SaaS (Software as a Service):   A subscription that is sold so that your customer can use your software.

Scaleable: How big your business can grow, how much market demand you have, and which markets you can grow into. A common question from investors is, "How scalable is this opportunity?" If you cannot scale, you might fall under the "cottage industry" or "lifestyle business" category.

Serial entrepreneur: Someone who launches a number of businesses, either simultaneously or one after another.

Rate Sheet

Here is a copy of my original and a standard rate sheet for Solid Ground Innovations. As your expertise grows you'll be able to charge a premium hourly rate.

You can download this from my website at https://www.sevetriwilson.com/.

Summary of Services		
On regarding how to price your services, please read the pricing chapter in Sevetri's book *Solid Ground: How I Built a 7 Figure Company at 22*		
(Company name) Staff Codes		
Employee/ Contractor 1	1.01 **Employee/ Contractor 5**	
Employee/ Contractor 2	1.02 **Employee/ Contractor 6**	1.06
Employee/ Contractor 3	1.03 **Employee/ Contractor 7**	1.07
Employee/ Contractor 4	1.04	

(Continued)

Summary of Services				
LINE ITEM	**(Staff Code-Hours)**	**Total Hours**	**Rate/hour**	Total
Content Development			$ 45.00	$ –
Partnership Development	(1.01-38)(1.04-35.25)(1.03-29)	102.25	$ 75.00	$ 7,668.75
Ongoing Implementation		50	$ 55.00	$ 2,750.00
Sustain-ability Planning			$ 125.00	$ –
Program Analysis			$ 95.00	$ –
Credits:				
(January Media Buying—Radio)				$ (3,768.00)
Total Monthly Billings				**$ 72,924.75**

Next is a sample of the deck that helped me raise $8 million in our Series A. The full version, along with the deck that helped us raise $2 million for our seed investment and $400,000 from our first investors, can be downloaded from https://www.sevetriwilson.com/.

Source: Network Effect, RATE SHEET, Resilia Creation. Retrieved from: https://www.sevetriwilson.com/.

Resilia's Investor Deck ——————————

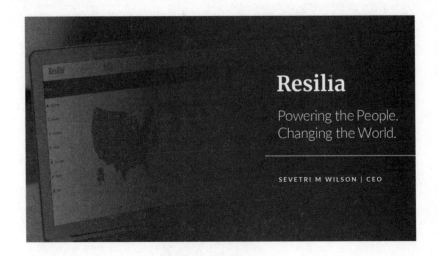

Resilia

Powering the People.
Changing the World.

SEVETRI M WILSON | CEO

The Result of Failure is Real

FAILURE MEANS:

- Failed projects
- High administrative costs
- Suffering communities
- Wasted investments
- Undelivered promises
- Misused public funds
- Bad PR
- Diminished funding chances

The Solution

RESILIA ALLOWS YOU TO...

- Scale your impact smarter and faster
- Streamline communication and ensure transparency
- Save time on annual reports and grantee onboarding
- Visualize your progress with customizable data displays

Network Effect

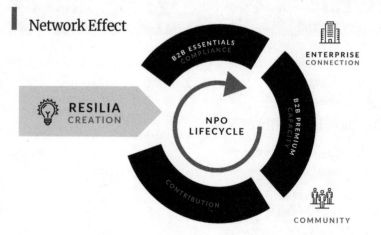

Online Resources

https://www.sevetriwilson.com/ (Go here for free downloads and resources delivered to your inbox via my weekly email.)

https://www.ycombinator.com/library (an extended library of terminology for startup founders)

https://www.sba.gov/funding-programs (a library of government programs and how to contract with the government. You can also find offices in every major city where you can schedule a free appointment with a program manager to understand your business needs.)

https://www.sbir.gov/ (SBIR, also known as Small Business Innovation Research, provides competitive funding to turn your R&D into products and services for global impact.)

https://firstround.com/review/ (In my opinion, one of the best, most useful newsletters for early-stage startups and founders.)

About
the Author

Sevetri Wilson is a serial entrepreneur and the founder of two companies, Solid Ground Innovations (SGI) and Resilia, a New Orleans-based technology startup with an office in New York City. Sevetri bootstrapped her first company, SGI, to seven figures with zero capital, and she raised $11 million for her second company, Resilia, which launched to the public in 2016. To date she has raised the most venture capital of any female founder from the state of Louisiana. In 2010, her work was recognized with the Nobel Prize for public service, the Jefferson Award, and was featured in the Senate report to the White House on volunteerism in America during the Obama administration. Sevetri has been featured in *Forbes*, *Black Enterprise*, *Essence*, *Inc.*, *Entrepreneur*, *USA Today*, CNN, and other news outlets for her work in business and technology. In 2019, she was named to *Inc.* magazine's 100 Women Building America's Most Innovative Companies list, PitchBook's top 27 Black Founders List, and Resilia to *Venture Beat*'s 10 Startups To Watch Outside of Silicon Valley. In 2020, she was named to the prestigious Forbes 100 Cloud List of Rising Stars. Sevetri splits her time between New Orleans and New York City.

She can be reached online at www.sevetriwilson.com or via social media @sevetriwilson.

Index